ICIW 2017

The Twelfth International Conference on Internet and Web Applications and Services

June 25 - 29, 2017

Venice, Italy

ICIW 2017 Editors

Paulo Caetano da Silva, Salvador University (UNIFACS), Brazil
Daniela Marghitu, Auburn University, USA

Printed from e-media with permission by:

Curran Associates, Inc.
57 Morehouse Lane
Red Hook, NY 12571

Some format issues inherent in the e-media version may also appear in this print version.

Printed by Curran Associates, Inc. (2017)

International Academy, Research, and Industry Association (IARIA)
412 Derby Way
Wilmington, DE 19810

Phone: (408) 893-6407
Fax: (408) 527-6351

petre@iaria.org

Additional copies of this publication are available from:

Curran Associates, Inc.
57 Morehouse Lane
Red Hook, NY 12571 USA
Phone: 845-758-0400
Fax: 845-758-2633
Email: curran@proceedings.com
Web: www.proceedings.com

TABLE OF CONTENTS

ICIW 2017

Forward

The Twelfth International Conference on Internet and Web Applications and Services (ICIW 2017), held between June 25-29, 2017 in Venice, Italy, continued a variety a series of co-located events that covered the complementary aspects related to designing and deploying of applications based on IP&Web techniques and mechanisms.

Internet and Web-based technologies led to new frameworks, languages, mechanisms and protocols for Web applications design and development. Interaction between web-based applications and classical applications requires special interfaces and exposes various performance parameters.

Web Services and applications are supported by a myriad of platforms, technologies, and mechanisms for syntax (mostly XML-based) and semantics (Ontology, Semantic Web). Special Web Services based applications such as e-Commerce, e-Business, P2P, multimedia, and GRID enterprise related, allow design flexibility and easy to develop new services. The challenges consist of service discovery, announcing, monitoring and management; on the other hand, trust, security, performance and scalability are desirable metrics under exploration when designing such applications.

Entertainment systems became one of the most business-oriented and challenging area of distributed real-time software applications' and special devices' industry. Developing entertainment systems and applications for a unique user or multiple users requires special platforms and network capabilities.

Particular traffic, QoS/SLA, reliability and high availability are some of the desired features of such systems. Real-time access raises problems of user identity, customized access, and navigation. Particular services such interactive television, car/train/flight games, music and system distribution, and sport entertainment led to ubiquitous systems. These systems use mobile, wearable devices, and wireless technologies.

Interactive game applications require particular methodologies, frameworks, platforms, tools and languages. State-of-the-art games today can embody the most sophisticated technology and the most fully developed applications of programming capabilities available in the public domain.

The impact on millions of users via the proliferation of peer-to-peer (P2P) file sharing networks such as eDonkey, Kazaa and Gnutella was rapidly increasing and seriously influencing business models (online services, cost control) and user behavior (download profile). An important fraction of the Internet traffic belongs to P2P applications.

P2P applications run in the background of user's PCs and enable individual users to act as downloaders, uploaders, file servers, etc. Designing and implementing P2P applications raise particular requirements. On the one hand, there are aspects of programming, data handling, and intensive computing applications; on the other hand, there are problems of special protocol features and networking, fault tolerance, quality of service, and application adaptability.

Additionally, P2P systems require special attention from the security point of view. Trust, reputation, copyrights, and intellectual property are also relevant for P2P applications. On-line communications frameworks and mechanisms allow distribute the workload, share business process, and handle complex partner profiles. This requires protocols supporting interactivity and realtime metrics.

Collaborative systems based on online communications support collaborative groups and are based on the theory and formalisms for group interactions. Group synergy in cooperative networks includes online gambling, gaming, and children groups, and at a larger scale, B2B and B2P cooperation.

Collaborative systems allow social networks to exist; within groups and between groups there are problems of privacy, identity, anonymity, trust, and confidentiality. Additionally, conflict, delegation, group selection, and communications costs in collaborative groups have to be monitored and managed. Building online social networks requires mechanism on popularity context, persuasion, as well as technologies, techniques, and platforms to support all these paradigms.

Also, the age of information and communication has revolutionized the way companies do business, especially in providing competitive and innovative services. Business processes not only integrates departments and subsidiaries of enterprises but also are extended across organizations and to interact with governments. On the other hand, wireless technologies and peer-to-peer networks enable ubiquitous access to services and information systems with scalability. This results in the removal of barriers of market expansion and new business opportunities as well as threats. In this new globalized and ubiquitous environment, it is of increasing importance to consider legal and social aspects in business activities and information systems that will provide some level of certainty. There is a broad spectrum of vertical domains where legal and social issues influence the design and development of information systems, such as web personalization and protection of users privacy in service provision, intellectual property rights protection when designing and implementing virtual works and multiplayer digital games, copyright protection in collaborative environments, automation of contracting and contract monitoring on the web, protection of privacy in location-based computing, etc.

The conference had the following tracks:

- Internet and Web-based Applications and Services
- Internet-based data, applications and services
- Virtual Environments and Web Applications for eLearning
- P2P Systems and Applications
- WFIS : Web Financial Information Systems

We take here the opportunity to warmly thank all the members of the ICIW 2017 technical program committee, as well as all the reviewers. The creation of such a high quality conference program would not have been possible without their involvement. We also kindly thank all the authors that dedicated much of their time and effort to contribute to ICIW 2017. We truly believe that, thanks to all these efforts, the final conference program consisted of top quality contributions.

We also gratefully thank the members of the ICIW 2017 organizing committee for their help in handling the logistics and for their work that made this professional meeting a success.

We hope that ICIW 2017 was a successful international forum for the exchange of ideas and results between academia and industry and to promote further progress in the field of Internet and Web applications and services. We also hope that Venice, Italy provided a pleasant environment during the conference and everyone saved some time to enjoy the unique charm of the city.

ICIW 2017 Chairs

ICIW Steering Committee

Stefanos Gritzalis, University of the Aegean, Greece
Sebastien Salva, UCA (Clermont Auvergne University), France
Raj Jain, Washington University in St. Louis, USA
Jian Yu, Auckland University of Technology, New Zealand
Christoph Meinel, Hasso-Plattner-Institut GmbH, Germany

ICIW Industry/Research Advisory Committee

José Luis Izkara, TECNALIA, Spain
Christos J. Bouras, University of Patras, Greece
Alex Ng, Internet Commerce Security Laboratory, Australia
Rema Hariharan, eBay, USA
Mustafa Rafique, IBM Research, Ireland

ICIW 2017
Committee

ICIW Steering Committee

Stefanos Gritzalis, University of the Aegean, Greece
Sebastien Salva, UCA (Clermont Auvergne University), France
Raj Jain, Washington University in St. Louis, USA
Jian Yu, Auckland University of Technology, New Zealand
Christoph Meinel, Hasso-Plattner-Institut GmbH, Germany

ICIW Industry/Research Advisory Committee

José Luis Izkara, TECNALIA, Spain
Christos J. Bouras, University of Patras, Greece
Alex Ng, Internet Commerce Security Laboratory, Australia
Rema Hariharan, eBay, USA
Mustafa Rafique, IBM Research, Ireland

ICIW 2017 Technical Program Committee

Mohd Helmy Abd Wahab, Universiti Tun Hussein Onn, Malaysia
Witold Abramowicz, Poznan University of Economics and Business, Poland
Mehmet Aktas, Yildiz Technical University, Turkey
Grigore Albeanu, Spiru Haret University - Bucharest, Romania
Markus Aleksy, ABB AG, Germany
Pedro Álvarez, University of Zaragoza, Spain
Filipe Araujo, University of Coimbra, Portugal
Ezzy Ariwa, University of Bedfordshire, UK
Jocelyn Aubert, Luxembourg Institute of Science and Technology (LIST), Luxembourg
Masoud Barati, Sherbrooke University, Canada
Andres Baravalle, University of East London, UK
Dan Benta, Agora University of Oradea, Romania
Luis Bernardo, Universidade NOVA de Lisboa, Portugal
Christos J. Bouras, University of Patras, Greece
Mahmoud Brahimi, University of Msila, Algeria
Paulo Caetano da Silva, Universidade Salvador - UNIFACS, Brazil
Jorge C. S. Cardoso, University of Coimbra, Portugal
Fernando Miguel Carvalho, ADEETC, ISEL - Polytechnic Institute of Lisbon, Portugal
Dickson Chiu, The University of Hong Kong, Hong Kong
Soon Ae Chun, City University of New York, USA
Marta Cimitile, Unitelma Sapienza University, Italy
Gianpiero Costantino, Institute of Informatics and Telematics (IIT) - National Research Council

(CNR), Italy
Giuseppe A. Di Lucca, University of Sannio | RCOST (Research Center on Software Technology), Italy
Ronaldo dos Santos Mello, Federal University of Santa Catarina, Brazil
Javier Fabra, Universidad de Zaragoza, Spain
Johannes Fähndrich, Technische Universität Berlin, Germany
Stefan Fischer, University of Lübeck, Germany
Karla Donato Fook, IFMA - Maranhao Federal Institute for Education, Science and Technology, Brazil
Panayotis Fouliras, University of Macedonia, Greece
Ivan Ganchev, University of Limerick, Ireland / Plovdiv University "Paisii Hilendarski", Bulgaria
Mohamed Gharzouli, University of Abdelhamid Mehri Constantine 2, Algeria
Nizar Ghoula, Yellow pages Group, Montreal, Canada
Katja Gilly de la Sierra - Llamazares, Universidad Miguel Hernández, Spain
Patrizia Grifoni, National Research Council, Italy
Stefanos Gritzalis, University of the Aegean, Greece
Carlos Guerrero, University of Balearic Islands, Spain
Bidyut Gupta, Southern Illinois University, USA
Ileana Hamburg, Institut Arbeit und Technik, Germany
Rema Hariharan, eBay, USA
Mamoun Abu Helou, Al Istiqlal University, Palestine
Martin Henkel, Stockholm University, Sweden
José Luis Herrero, University of Extremadura, Spain
Tzung-Pei Hong, National University of Kaohsiung, Taiwan
Arthur Huang, Tarleton State University, USA
Emilio Insfran, Universitat Politecnica de Valencia, Spain
Naghmeh Ivaki, University of Coimbra, Portugal
José Luis Izkara, TECNALIA, Spain
Raj Jain, Washington University in St. Louis, USA
Marc Jansen, University of Applied Sciences Ruhr West, Germany
Jehn-Ruey Jiang, National Central University, Taiwan
Dimitris Karagiannis, University of Vienna, Austria
Sokratis K. Katsikas, Center for Cyber & Information Security | Norwegian University of Science & Technology (NTNU), Norway
Selma Khouri, ESI, Algeria / ENSMA, France
Suhyun Kim, KIST (Korea Institute of Science and Technology), South Korea
Samad Kolahi, Unitec Institute of Technology, New Zealand
George Koutromanos, National and Kapodistrian University of Athens, Greece
Sarasi Lalithsena, Kno.e.sis Center | Wright State University, USA
José Laurindo Campos dos Santos, Instituto Nacional de Pesquisas da Amazônia, Brazil
Longzhuang Li, Texas A&M University-Corpus Christi, USA
Lei Liu, HP Labs, USA
David Lizcano Casas, Open University of Madrid (UDIMA), Spain
Malamati Louta, University of Western Macedonia, Greece

Copyright Information

Towards Exploratory Search Mashups based on Strategic Knowledge

Oliver Mroß, Carsten Radeck and Klaus Meißner

Faculty of Computer Science
Technische Universität Dresden
Dresden, Germany
Email: {oliver.mross, carsten.radeck, klaus.meissner}@tu-dresden.de

Abstract—**Exploratory search is a complex, long-lasting and highly iterative process. Users may have only a vague or an open-ended information need that is likely to change during the search process. Besides the insufficient domain knowledge, most users lack experience in efficient information search. Hence, they have to be guided during the search process by strategic recommendations. In this work, we present an overview of our strategy-oriented search platform that derives appropriate composite web applications from recommended and preferred search strategies with respect to the current user and search context. Moreover, we give a glimpse into our meta-model of search strategies, which represent best practices on how to solve search problems and are described using hierarchical task models.**

Keywords–Mashup; End-User Development; Exploratory Search; Search Strategy; Strategy Recommendation.

I. Introduction

Considering today's vast amount of digital information and it's increasing availability, information search is an omnipresent human activity [1]. Traditional Web search engines follow the same retrieval paradigm "query and response". Thereby, the user's information need is represented as a keyword-based query that is processed by the search engine. Corresponding results are returned as a ranked list of entities containing additional meta-data, e. g., title, content fragments and the data source. However, this lookup-oriented information seeking model does not fully represent the human search behavior in real life scenarios. Users may have a vague or open-ended information need, which furthermore is likely to change during the search process. Satisfying his/her information need is additionally hindered if the user's research or domain expertise are insufficient [2]. Consequently, *exploratory search* characterizes information seeking as a highly iterative, often long-lasting and complex process [3]. As pointed out by [4], assisting users during the search process is crucial. We argue the searcher has to be guided by *search strategies*, which are consolidated, verified and composable best practices on how to solve search problems. To this end, search strategies are recommended by the search environment and serve as foundation for generating dashboard-like search applications with respect to the current context (i. e., user's profile, search history, research task description and problem domain).

A promising approach for generating context-aware search dashboards are *composite web applications* (CWA) consisting of loosely coupled *mashup components*. The latter encapsulate arbitrary web-services and resources like domain-specific business logic as well as widgets. Moreover, each component is characterized by a semantically enriched interface providing information according to their data provision and capabilities [5]. It has the advantage that a component's interface as well as their capabilities can be matched more precisely on a semantic level with an abstract application description including required capabilities, e. g., a business process model, and allows to generate corresponding mashups.

In our vision, a *search strategy* is a formal description of the planned use of information gathering activities leading effectively and efficiently to relevant search results. An information gathering activity is performed by the user, e. g., providing an author's name, or by the search system, for instance, presenting the author's books or papers relevant to the user's information need. A search strategy is effective because the resulting entities (documents, terms, domains etc.) are highly relevant compared to the user's information need. It is efficient because it reduces the user's cognitive load by providing a predefined order of search activities and it reduces the amount of time in finding relevant information.

The idea is to utilize strategy models for assisting users throughout search processes. Thereby, strategies are recommended context-sensitively, giving advice on efficient search activities. Additionally, they serve as a foundation to derive adequate CWA, taking advantage of composition knowledge and the semantic description of component interfaces.

Typically, strategies are associated to a critical situation and should result in valuable information related to the initial search problem. Consider the following two strategy examples:

1) "Define the information need more precisely by selecting refined concepts of domain X using archive services $S_1, S_2, \ldots, S_n$ if precision level of current query is low."
2) "Reformulate a query more precisely by searching for concepts in top-10 relevant papers and slides of domain experts $E_1, E_2, \ldots, E_m$ if the user's search experience is low and the current result list is almost empty."

Such search strategies are defined explicitly by search experts or can be derived semi-automatically from usage and feedback data of experienced searchers.

Our vision of a guided exploratory search experience comes with various requirements. First, a sufficiently expressive *search strategy meta-model* for describing stepwise information gathering processes usable in a multitude of scenarios is needed. It should address the following aspects: (a) Specifying *information request and provision activities*, concrete domain concepts or placeholders, each referencing a domain concept, a document type or a human informant (e. g., the data analysis expert) are needed. (b) *Context criteria* to define valid usage situations of search strategies are required considering the temporal availability and validity of multidimensional context data. Secondly, the meta-model concepts are the basis for *strategy recommendation* and *mashup generation*, i. e., the concepts should largely support the component selection and composition process to reduce the configuration effort from the end-user perspective. Considering that there is a semantic gap between the abstract process-oriented strategy meta-model and the fine-grained, function-oriented model of mashup components, there is a need for an *efficient mapping algorithm* that should be executed transparently during the search process.

Regarding the previous requirements, the contributions of this work are the following: First, we propose a meta-model for search strategies that allows to specify arbitrarily complex information gathering activities and which features semantic annotations. Second, we present a novel reference architecture of an exploratory search platform. It supports unexperienced users in highly iterative information search with help of guidance mechanisms leveraging the strategy meta-model. Especially users are assisted by strategy recommendation and provision of adequate search mashups. The remainder of this paper is structured as follows. In Section II, we discuss related work. Then, Section III presents our search platform based on mashup concepts. Finally, Section IV concludes the paper.

II. Related Work

Approaches like query suggestion [4], [6] and facet recommendation [7], [8] try to compensate the limited domain and search expertise of users. Such techniques are assisting users in specifying an information need more precisely. However, users often have complex information needs requiring them to perform multiple search steps [9]. Such approaches fall short of expectations in supporting users on a strategic level.

Kangasrääsiö et al. [10] propose a search front-end showing estimates of the user's search action effects allowing the user to anticipate consequences and to direct his/her exploratory search. Thus, the user actively influences the information search. Musetti et al. [11] use topological knowledge patterns extracted from Wikipedia to deliver relevant and filtered search results. Each result is represented semantically and visualized based on concepts provided by DBpedia. Complementing meta-data are retrieved from additional sources such as Twitter. Anyway, for users without extensive domain knowledge, it is challenging to navigate to relevant information. We follow the motive of [10], but we argue that users without guidance explore information rather in a trial and error manner. Thus, information search still is time consuming and cumbersome. Compared to our solution, both approaches lack concepts for active user guidance.

Bates describes four levels of search activities [12], whereby higher levels build upon lower ones. *Moves* are the basic unit of her model. *Tactics* are composed of moves in order to improve search activities. *Stratagems* are larger complexes of several moves or tactics and they are typically domain-specific. A *strategy* can be considered as a plan for a whole search process, incorporating all other types of activities. Bates emphasizes the importance of supporting users on strategic levels, which is one of the main goals of our approach. In contrast to [12], we formally describe search activities of all levels. Belkin characterize *information seeking strategies* (ISS) [13] according to the dimensions: *method* of interaction, *goal* of interaction, *mode* of retrieval, and resource considered. They identify 16 relevant combinations and thus strategies. Our model is partly inspired by this work, as we describe user's situation and search activities. However, it lacks formalism and a detailed search process description. In [14] Belkin et al. propose script-based user guidance, whereby scripts represent effective interaction sequences for ISS. Such scripts serve as prototypical dialogs between system and user and can be combined to more complex ones. In the case of the *MERIT* platform [14], scripts guide users during the search process. Besides initially provided scripts, case-based reasoning is applied to derive scripts. Similarly, our approach allows to model circumstances when a strategy can be applied. However, we take the information need and user group into consideration. In addition, we describe search processes, yet in a semantically enriched and user-oriented way.

According to Sutcliffe and Ennis [15], strategies represent information searching skills and are determined by the type of information need. The latter is categorized according to aspects like the knowledge a user has about the information, whether the need is rather fix or likely to change, and if the target is precisely known or rather general. They propose a search process model that features strategy selection rules, which govern behavior within the process model. Such rules differ in their preconditions, incorporating information need types and other context parameters, as well as action clauses that, e. g., alter the query and invoke an action. Strategy rules are used to determine suitable strategies with respect to the information need type and current search process. Our approach is influenced by the work of Sutcliff and Ennis. For instance, we adopt their concepts for describing information needs and context-sensitively selecting suitable strategies in a rule-based manner. However, they provide no model of strategic process knowledge as we require it.

The *FIRE* system presented in [16] offers strategic help to users in form of suggestions, which partially correspond to Bates' classification. They apply reasoning on user actions and the search context to derive applicable suggestions. Selecting suggestions is based on rules describing necessary context conditions and the consequences as actions. Our approach not only allows to provide suggestions in context of a predefined search application, but also uses strategic knowledge to derive suitable applications, which is out of scope of FIRE. In addition, our strategy model can describe whole search processes and strategies can be composed. Kriewel et al. present *DAFFODIL* [9] that uses case-based reasoning techniques for determining appropriate strategic suggestions considering the current user's context based on the tactics and stratagems according to [12]. Tacke and Kriewel [2] extend DAFFODIL by providing tools enabling guided information search. They differentiate between macro and micro-level guidance. The former support unexperienced users in specifying his/her information need and explaining steps of a complex search task. A disadvantage is a fixed set of generic features and tools for the different search process phases. Domain-specific visualizations and user preferences are considered in a very limited fashion only. Our platform strives to provide strategic knowledge and a construction kit to reflect it in suitable CWA.

III. Strategy-oriented Search Platform

In this section, first we present an architectural overview of our CWA platform for exploratory search and its strategy-based functionalities. Afterwards, details on our proposed strategy model are discussed. Finally, we describe some of the novel features, which utilize strategy models.

A. Architectural Overview

We claim that assistance mechanisms based on formalized strategy descriptions, for instance, context-aware strategy recommendations, generation of appropriate applications and query suggestions, are supporting and substantially simplifying the user's overall search process. As result of our investigation of related solutions (see Section II) and to the best of our knowledge, there is a need for a novel information search platform providing such assistance, which we present afterwards.

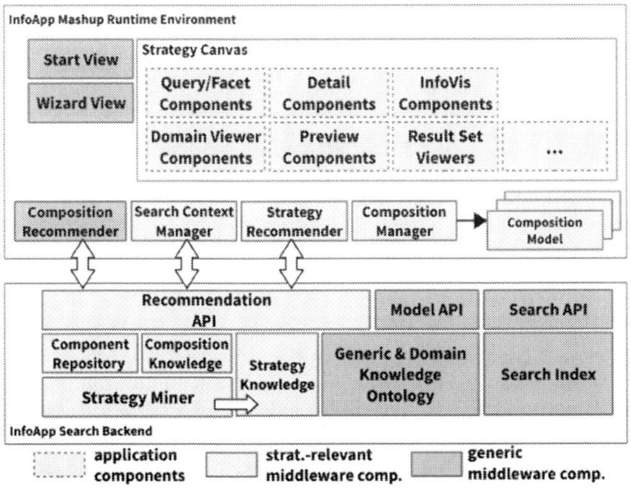

Figure 1. Architectural overview of our platform for exploratory search.

As illustrated in Figure 1, the search platform's front-end is based on a mashup runtime environment. The *composition manager* implements the life-cycle of CWA, which are represented by a *composition model*. Exploratory search mashups are rendered in the *strategy canvas* and build up on a set of components that provide capabilities to cover all phases of a search process, for instance, components for textual or graphical query construction, result lists and diagrams as well as charts for visual analytics. In order to provide several starting points into the research process, the front-end provides a *start view* and a *wizard*, c.f. Section III-C. The platform features a component-oriented recommender system (*composition recommender*) and assistance mechanisms for live development of CWA [5]. They allow to recommend, select and compose components as required. To this end, *composition knowledge*, that holds information about mashups and recurring composition patterns, and a *component repository*, that stores information about semantically annotated components, are utilized. Both are accessible via the *recommendation API*. In addition, the latter provides the following context-aware search-oriented recommendation functionalities: (a) suggest domain concepts and facets, (b) suggest query reformulations, (c) recommend related documents, domains and their inherent concepts, and (d) recommend search strategies each associated with at least one adequate CWA. These functions incorporate domain knowledge represented in *ontologies*. Furthermore, they pay attention to the current search context, which comprises a users' research task, queries, information need and skills. It is maintained by the *search context manager* and analyzed by the recommender in order to fulfill the above mentioned functionalities. *Strategy knowledge* serves as a further crucial data source for our recommendation and assistance features. Therein, formal models of search strategies according to our meta-model, see Section III-B, are stored and maintained. A *strategy miner* is responsible for semi-automatically detecting recurring work-flows in the *composition knowledge*. By comparing the current context with the purpose and use cases of a search strategy, the *strategy recommender* derives and presents suitable strategies, as detailed in Section III-C.

In order to answer user queries, search mashups leverage the *search API*, which grants access to our hybrid *search index*. The latter combines the efficiency of an inverted index together with the expressiveness of an ontology.

B. Strategy Model

As a prerequisite, we briefly outline our *user and search context model*. Therein, user profiles model skills that include search and domain expertise, and interests based on semantic concepts and quality levels. Users have certain *roles*, that additionally imply specific skills and can group users. Furthermore, the current search context describes the search task featuring a textual description, research goals (adopting [13]) associated with semantic domain concepts, a classification of the information need (based on [15]). Further, current research activities including a history of queries and gathered feedback of users in association to relevant documents, concepts or strategies is represented.

Search strategies describe effective, proven practices for fulfilling certain information needs, for instance, searching patents by navigating in a classification or by querying companies in a sector. According to our meta-model depicted in Figure 2, each *search strategy* is formally characterized by the following attributes.

- *core meta-data* like a name and description
- circumstances (*cases*) under which a strategy is useful. Such cases are basically tuples of *search task*, user *roles* and *rating*, reflecting the suitability of a strategy in a given context. To describe target groups of users for that a strategy is suitable, we utilize user *roles*, that group users with respect to their skills. Furthermore, a case is associated with a model of a CWA. There are two types of cases differing in their origin:
    - *reference purposes* are defined by search experts,
    - *community feedback* on the suitability of strategies.
- hierarchical task model (*search strategy* and subclasses) formally specifying a procedural description including
    - place holders carrying selection rules for dynamic expansion using other strategy models (see *isTemplate*),
    - composite and/or conditional activities (expressed in sequential or parallel order or as alternatives). Hierarchically defined *conditions* allow to further restrict when strategies are applicable. Therein, arbitrary context parameters are addressable using a selector language, like SPARQL property paths.
    - besides user actions, activities can model system actions and thus configure platform features similar to [15], like the recommender system and the component selection during CWA generation.

As can be seen, our model is influenced by cases and scripts [14], task models and capabilities [5]. With regard to Bates' categorization, our model covers all levels, i. e., it is capable of describing moves, tactics and arbitrarily complex stratagems and strategies.

C. Strategy-based Platform Features

As indicated in Figure 3, we distinguish two roles interacting with our platform. *Users* with little or no strategic

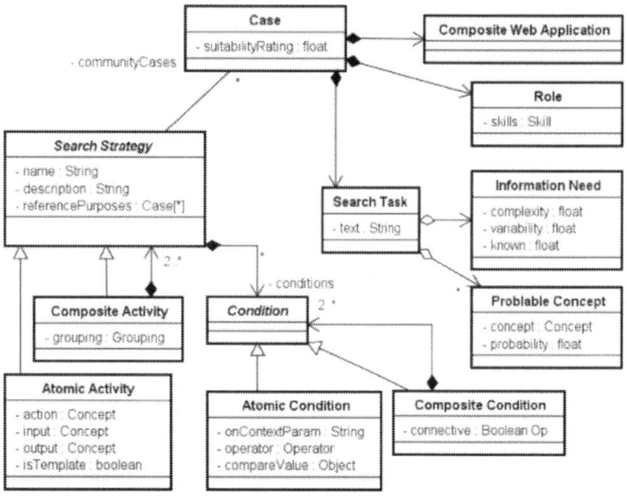

Figure 2. Overview of the search strategy meta-model.

expertise and with limited domain knowledge utilize our platform to fulfill their information need. *Search experts* are experienced information seekers with profound knowledge about efficient search strategies, which they apply as required. To this end, they create or modify CWA on demand. We assume, that experts are interested in sharing strategic knowledge by explicitly modeling their strategies and contributing them to the platform's strategy knowledge.

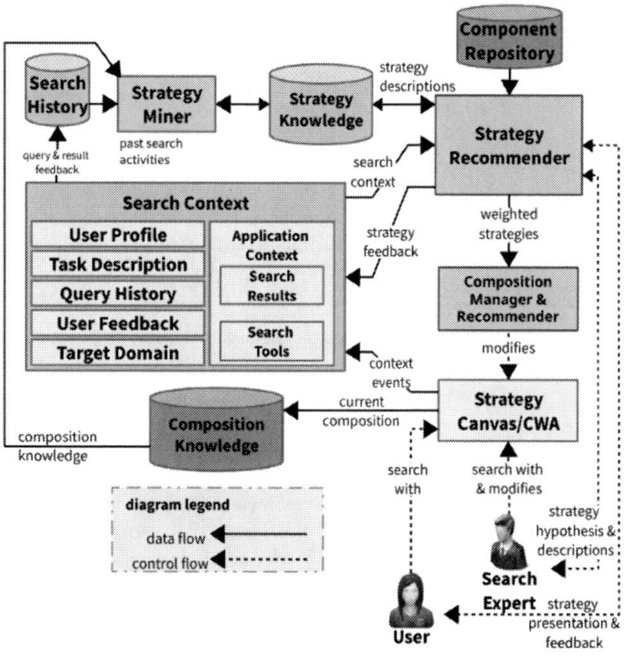

Figure 3. Strategy Recommendation Overview

In our approach the search platform provides following main features, which we explain in more detail afterwards:

Strategy assignment: Search strategies are assigned to matching CWA automatically by the *strategy miner* prior to the user's information search. Furthermore, the *search expert* can specify the association between a strategy and its representing application semi-automatically at runtime.

Strategy recommendation: Search strategies are recommended by the *strategy recommender* at the *beginning* or *during* the search process. For this, meta-data, e. g., the name and human readable description, are visualized by the *wizard* or as part of the *search canvas*.

Strategy usage: After strategies were recommended, the user activates the most appropriate strategy. At this point, the association between the selected strategy and its referenced CWA is resolved. Thereafter, we consider following integration cases: (a) Initial setup of the CWA, (b) extend or (c) replace the current composition.

Strategy feedback: From the user's perspective a strategy leads to more or less suitable search results. Reusing a valuable strategy or to filter out unsuitable ones the user can give feedback.

Next, we discuss these features considering the relations between actors and platform entities depicted in Figure 3.

Strategy assignment: We distinguish between *automatic* and *semi-automatic* strategy assignments. The latter is performed by *search experts*. In the first case, the *strategy miner* compares each registered strategy model with available CWAs managed by the *composition knowledge base* in association with historical context parameters provided by the *search history*, e. g., the research task or user profile. When comparing the strategy and CWA, the strategy's context condition are matched with context parameters associated to the current mashup. Moreover, the strategy's activities are compared with capability descriptions of each component referenced in the mashup's composition. Both values—the *context* and *activity* matching degree— result in the overall strategy-application similarity. After a strategy has been matched with available CWAs, the applications list is ranked with respect to the matching degree of every strategy-application pair. The top-k applications are associated with the current strategy using the *case* concept introduced in Section III-B and stored in the *strategy knowledge base*. In summary, each strategy is compared with available CWA and the best matching applications per strategy are assigned. The associated applications are considered as the strategy's manifestation on the application layer and are advertised during the user's search time.

In the case of *semi-automatic* strategy assignment, while the *search expert* is composing an information search mashup the *strategy miner* calculates probable strategies at runtime. At this, the expert's mashup as well as his/her search context are compared to each strategy model similarly to the algorithm described above. As result, probable strategies are calculated and visualized as *hypothetic candidates* to *search experts*. The latter evaluate strategy-application pairs and can modify strategy models and CWA, for instance, add domain and knowledge conditions as well as domain-specific mashup components. Thus, the validity and relevance of strategies is ensured by explicit feedback and the expertise of search professionals.

Strategy recommendation: Essentially, our platform provides two entry points into the search process: In the *start view* users can browse recommended strategies, which are filtered with respect to the user profile, or is guided by a *wizard*. The latter supports users in formulating research goals, captures relevant topics and assists users by recommending related search strategies. In addition, default search CWA for generic strategies can quickly be accessed. Initial strategy recommendations take into account the user context with skills, roles and history, and the search context including task description, information need and queries. The *strategy recommender* derives suitable strategies leveraging semantic filtering techniques. For this, context conditions of every strategy are evaluated and matched with current context parameters. For example, the strategy "find chemical patents by formular" includes following conditions: $((domain \simeq \text{chemistry}) \vee (userrole \simeq \text{patent officer}))$. As fallback solutions there are general purpose strategies and corresponding CWA featuring generic search tools.

Further, strategies are recommended at *runtime*. To enable guidance throughout search processes, the current context is continuously monitored. Upon relevant context changes, e. g., modified query, selected target domains and facets etc., new loops of the recommendation procedure are triggered. Consider the following example: After the user has selected several documents and topics from the chemistry domain, the platform offers matching strategies. One of them—strategy "precise chemical search queries"—suggests to use a chemistry-specific query formulation tool based on chemical formulas. As soon as the user accepts, assigned CWAs are presented as sorted list in the strategy canvas. The applications order depends on the similarity of each strategy-application pair and on the feedback of other users or search experts. The *case's suitability rating* introduced in Section III-B represents both aspects.

Strategy usage: After recommendation, a user can choose from several strategies and at least a CWA per selected strategy is generated. At this point, we differentiate between following integration cases. At the *beginning* of the search process, the *strategy canvas* only includes generic search tools such as a query editor, a facet browser and a search results viewer. Per selected strategy the user can activate most appropriate mashups and decides whether the current composition will be extended or a new mashup is created in the *strategy canvas*. After the user has chosen an option, components and communication relations between them are integrated as defined in the composition model associated to the activated strategy. The integration process is performed and monitored by the *composition manager*.

Moreover, strategies are recommended continuously throughout the search process. Hence, while using an activated strategy a recommended one can be *merged* into the existing application context. A sample strategy is presented in Figure 4. Activities and conditions of the search strategy "SUPER" are shown as UML state diagram. Context conditions are visualized as transition guards. For instance, the main strategy "SUPER" is suggested when there are less or equal than five search results and when the current query is overspecified. The strategy's purpose is to support users in finding appropriate hypernyms. For this, the main strategy contains two activities. First activity "Select" results in a hypernym that is automatically set as the current query (second "Modify" activity). As discussed in Section III-B our meta-model supports to define template activities, which could be replaced by more specific variants at runtime. In Figure 4 the first activity is replaced with a domain-specific one (green colored), which is activated after the user has selected the chemistry domain. The new strategy allows retrieving chemical formulas from several sources, e. g., a query from search history or a web-service, and to get an appropriate hypernym from a chosen chemical formula. The selected hypernym is used to solve the problem of overspecified queries and to broaden the search results. Modifications on the strategy's activity layer are synchronized with the mashup's composition layer. Considering the sample strategy in Figure 4, generic composition fragments are replaced with domain-specific components.

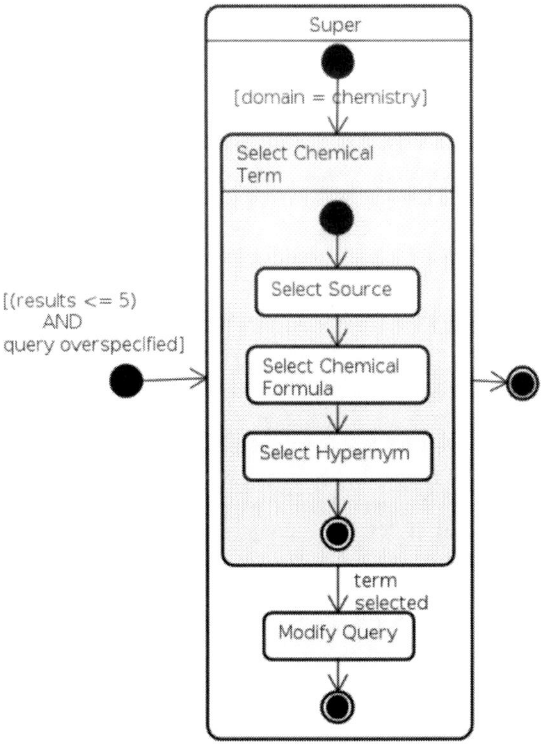

Figure 4. Sample strategy SUPER

Strategy feedback: At this point, we distinguish between *search expert* and *user* feedback on a strategy and its CWA. It is collected and managed by the *strategy recommender*. Feedback is created as a tuple of strategy, CWA, user and search context and represented as *case* stored by the *strategy knowledge base*. When more users give positive feedback according to the same case, the higher the corresponding strategy is weighted, i. e., its suitability rating increases. This in turn causes a higher ranking of the strategy during the recommendation process. Negatively rated strategies are degraded.

IV. CONCLUSIONS

In addition to the insufficient domain expertise, most users lack experience in efficient information search. Thus, there is a need for an intelligent search platform guiding the searcher by recommending appropriate search strategies. We support the user in his/her information seeking activities by continuously recommending collaboratively filtered search strategies depending on the current search context, so the user is able to design his/her CWA only by selecting a preferred strategy description. Further, search experts can teach valid search strategies to the platform. Users of the same community may profit from their expertise, because the platform is able to derive best matching compositions that the experts themselves can not anticipate during their search activities.

However, limitations of the presented approach are (a) the *cold start problem* and (b) the user's *cognitive overload* while using complex search strategies with deep activity hierarchies.

The first limitation is characterized by the necessity to provide predefined strategy descriptions and composition models. Hence, we introduced the *search expert* as actor with sufficient information seeking and programming experience who can explicitly specify strategy models. In order to reduce the inherent cognitive load and time effort, sophisticated strategy development tools that allow designing strategies comfortably are required. For this, a visual editor based on UML activity diagram notations could be used to generate reusable strategy models. Another approach would be to extract strategies from existing CWA automatically. For this, tracking features to capture the expert's input and interaction events as entities of the application context are required. In addition, sufficient analyses and aggregation mechanisms to recognize strategic search decisions from user behavioral patterns are required. Considering black-box components that have app-like granularity, this is not feasible due to missing interaction details. Thus, we decided to rely on (semi-)automatic assignment of adequate CWA to strategies, but this implies that there are always corresponding mashups available. We assume there are several predefined compositions models, which are developed by domain experts without programming experience using EUD-tools [5]. Our platform supports the mashup EUD, but currently lacks the strategy assignment features described above. In the near future, we plan to develop the *strategy miner* and its strategy assignment features as part of the existing *composition and component repository* web-service of the platform's back-end.

The second limitation could be solved using automatically generated tutorials, which give an overview of integrated mashup components and are guiding users while interacting with them. For instance, in the chemistry domain they describe how a chemical formula editor is used in combination with the facet browser and a graph-like molecule viewer of the same application. Based on the assumption that such tutorials are generated from strategy knowledge and additional component interface annotations (e. g., capability descriptions) this solution complicates component development.

Finally, we plan to evaluate our approach with the help of a user study.

Acknowledgements

This work is funded as result of the InfoApp-project (https://mmt.inf.tu-dresden.de/infoapp) by the European Union and the Free State of Saxony within the EFRE program.

References

[1] G. Marchionini and R. White, "Find what you need, understand what you find," International Journal of Human–Computer Interaction, vol. 23, no. 3, 2007, p. 205–237.

[2] A. Tacke and S. Kriewel, "Strategic search support on macro and micro level," Datenbank Spectrum, vol. 14, no. 1, 2014, p. 19–28.

[3] R. White and R. Roth, Exploratory Search:Beyond the Query-Response Paradigm. Morgan & Claypool, 2009.

[4] A. Hassan Awadallah, R. W. White, P. Pantel, S. T. Dumais, and Y.-M. Wang, "Supporting complex search tasks," in Proceedings of the 23rd ACM International Conference on Conference on Information and Knowledge Management, ser. CIKM '14. New York, NY, USA: ACM, 2014, p. 829–838.

[5] C. Radeck, G. Blichmann, and K. Meißner, "Estimating the functionality of mashup applications for assisted, capability-centered end user development," in Proceedings of the 12th International Conference on Web Information Systems and Technologies (WEBIST 2016), 2016, pp. 109–120.

[6] D. Jiang, K. W.-T. Leung, L. Yang, and W. Ng, "Query suggestion with diversification and personalization," Knowledge-Based Systems, vol. 89, 2015, p. 553–568.

[7] M. Tvarožek and M. Bieliková, "Generating exploratory search interfaces for the semantic web," in Human-Computer Interaction. Springer, 2010, p. 175–186.

[8] T. Le, B. Vo, and T. H. Duong, "Personalized facets for semantic search using linked open data with social networks," in Innovations in Bio-Inspired Computing and Applications (IBICA), 2012 Third International Conference on. IEEE, 2012, pp. 312–317.

[9] S. Kriewel and N. Fuhr, "Evaluation of an adaptive search suggestion system," in European Conference on Information Retrieval. Springer, 2010, p. 544–555.

[10] A. Kangasrääsiö, D. Glowacka, and S. Kaski, "Improving controllability and predictability of interactive recommendation interfaces for exploratory search," in Proceedings of the 20th international conference on intelligent user interfaces. ACM, 2015, pp. 247–251.

[11] A. Musetti, A. G. Nuzzolese, F. Draicchio, V. Presutti, E. Blomqvist, A. Gangemi, and P. Ciancarini, "Aemoo: Exploratory search based on knowledge patterns over the semantic web," Semantic Web Challenge, vol. 136, 2012.

[12] M. J. Bates, "Where should the person stop and the information search interface start?" Information Processing & Management, vol. 26, no. 5, 1990, p. 575–591.

[13] N. Belkin, P. Marchetti, and C. Cool, "Braque: Design of an interface to support user interaction in information retrieval," Information Processing & Management, vol. 29, no. 3, 1993, p. 325–344.

[14] N. J. Belkin, C. Cool, A. Stein, and U. Thiel, "Cases, scripts, and information-seeking strategies: On the design of interactive information retrieval systems," Expert Systems with Applications, vol. 9, no. 3, 1995, p. 379–395.

[15] A. Sutcliffe and M. Ennis, "Towards a cognitive theory of information retrieval," Interacting with Computers, vol. 10, no. 3, 1998, p. 321 – 351.

[16] G. Brajnik, S. Mizzaro, C. Tasso, and F. Venuti, "Strategic help in user interfaces for information retrieval," Journal of the Association for Information Science and Technology, vol. 53, no. 5, 2002, pp. 343–358.

[17] C. Radeck, A. Lorz, G. Blichmann, and K. Meißner, "Hybrid Recommendation of Composition Knowledge for End User Development of Mashups," in ICIW 2012, The Seventh International Conference on Internet and Web Applications and Services, 2012, pp. 30–33.

Towards Validation of IFC Models with IfcDoc and SWRL

A Comparative Study

Muhammad Fahad
Centre Scientifique et Technique du Bâtiment
290 Route des Lucioles,
Sophia Antipolis 06904, France
fahad.muhammad@cstb.fr

Nicolas Bus, Franck Andrieux
Centre Scientifique et Technique du Bâtiment
290 Route des Lucioles,
Sophia Antipolis 06904, France
{firstname.lastname}@cstb.fr

Abstract—**Recent years have witnessed the need of automatic verification requirements to warn the non-conformities with the associated 3D visualization, or to provide access to the technical documentation for a given digital model based on its sophisticated contextual information. In this paper, we study two approaches for the validation of IFC Models, i.e., with IfcDoc and SWRL. The traditional approach is by using IfcDoc tool developed by buildingSMART International to improve the consistent and computer-interpretable definition of Model View Definitions. On the other hand, Semantic Web technologies, especially Semantic Web rule language, allow the semantic validation of IFC models to enable the compliance checking of IFC construction models with unmatchable query performance and flexibility. Therefore, we present and compare IfcDoc and Semantic Web rule language technologies for the model instance verification and conformance checking of IFC models, and demonstrate various important aspects and their limitations. We conclude that both technologies have their specific significances, but Semantic Web technologies provide a better hand over the traditional approach. The Semantic Web approach with the goal of combining the strengths of an ontology and IFC technologies makes information retrieval from an IFC model faster, flexible and also enables interoperability between IFC documents.**

Keywords-Validation of IFC models; SWRL; Ontology; BIM; Querying IFC models; MVDXML.

I. INTRODUCTION

To understand a building through the usage of a digital model which draws on a range of data assembled collaboratively before, during and after construction is referred to as Building Information Modeling (BIM) [1]. It brings together all the information about every component of a building, in one place. BIM with its interoperability properties is intended to facilitate exchanges and handovers between different stakeholders. While the visualization and geometric representation are intrinsic to the digital building model, the fields of quality requirements, evaluation and regulatory contextualization (destination, named areas, threshold values, certified data, evidence of compliance, etc.) need higher level of maturity [2]. Industry Foundation Classes (IFC) is the complete and fully stable open and international standard for exchanging BIM data [3]. Building SMART organization aims at publishing IFC and related buildingSMART data model standards. The buildingSMART data model standards are developed by the Model Support Group, and the implementation activities are coordinated by the Implementation Support Group [4]. Together, both groups organize the IFC software certification process. It aims to be a global standard for the BIM data exchange. The subset of the IFC schema needed to satisfy one or many Exchange Requirements of the Architecture, Engineering and Construction (AEC) industry is called Model View Definitions (MVD). The XML format used to publish the concepts and associated rules is MVDXML and it is regarded as an open standard [5]. MVDs provide additional rules for the IFC validation and focus on extracting integral model subsets for the IFC implementation purposes. There are many drawbacks of MVDXML for extracting building views such as: lack of logical formalisms, solely consideration of IFC schema and MVD-based view constructors are not very flexible and dynamic [6]. Although IFC is an open standard, its complex nature makes the information retrieval difficult from an IFC model, and thus affects the validation process by MVDXML rules. Many tasks for IFC model such as information retrieval, model validation, etc., do not achieve real-time performance in the real-world BIM scenarios.

Our enterprise, Centre Scientifique et Technique du Bâtiment (CSTB), through its research and development efforts, aims at automatic validation requirements to warn the non-conformities with the associated 3D visualization, or to provide access to the technical documentation for a given digital model based on its sophisticated contextual information. To achieve these goals, our research adopts a traditional approach using MVDXML [5] and, in addition, focuses on the Semantic Web rule language SWRL [7] for the validation of IFC construction and building models. The traditional approach by using IfcDoc tool developed by buildingSMART International is to improve the consistent and computer-interpretable definition of MVD as true subsets of the IFC Specification with the enhanced definition of concepts. Therefore, first, we present background knowledge about both these approaches and then compare IfcDoc and SWRL technologies for the model instance verification and conformance checking of IFC models. In addition, we demonstrate various important aspects and their limitation as well. We also performed experiments via queries by the traditional approach via IfcDoc and the ontology-based Resource Description Framework (RDF) approach IFC-to-RDF via SPARQL queries [8]. IFC-to-RDF is a set of reusable Java component that allows parsing IFC-SPF files and converts them into RDF graphs. Our approach uses IFC to RDF conversion and then stores RDF triples into Stardog [9] knowledge graph that gives unmatched query performance. We investigated that IFC; although is an open standard, it has a complex nature which makes information retrieval difficult from an IFC model. On the other hand, Semantic Web technologies, especially SWRL, allow for the semantic verification of IFC models to enable the compliance checking of IFC construction models with fast querying performance.

The rest of paper is organized as follows. Section 2 provides the background knowledge of the domain. Section 3 presents the related work. Section 4 presents two approaches for the validation of rules and conformance checking. Section 5 discusses our experimental findings via MVDXML validation rules on IfcDoc and SPARQL queries. Section 6 concludes this paper.

II. Background

In this section, we provide some background about the two approaches that can be used for the validation of IFC models.

A. *IfcDoc Tool and MVDXML*

The subset of the IFC schema needed to satisfy one or many Exchange Requirements of the Architecture, Engineering and Construction (AEC) industry is called *Model View Definition* (MVD). The XML format used to publish the concepts and associated rules is MVDXML and it is regarded as an open standard [5]. MVDs provide additional rules for the IFC validation and focus on extracting integral model subsets for IFC implementation purposes. The buildingSMART is willing to support construction domain developers in reusing its leading openBIM standard IFC as a baseline to set up specific data exchange protocols to satisfy exchange requirements in the industry. The buildingSMART International has developed IfcDoc tool for creating Model View Definitions. Based on the newly developed mvdXML standard, just Model View Definitions can now be easily developed using the IfcDoc tool. The tool and methodology can be applied to all IFC releases (IFC2x3, IFC4, etc.). For the validation of an IFC file against a particular model view, IfcDoc tool user interface displays a pane on the right side containing object instances within the file matching definitions selected in the tree view. The end-user can generate a report in the HTML format indicating if the file is valid according to the specified model view, and detailing what passes or fails. However, it does not show the cause or provide mechanisms for reasoning the inconsistencies or anomalies.

B. *SWRL and SQWRL*

The Semantic Web technologies, SWRL and SQWRL, are widely being used for the inference of new knowledge, validation and querying ontologies [7]. Ontologies, although they are best for knowledge modeling, have limitations and may not suffice for all applications. There are statements that cannot be expressed in Ontology Web Language; therefore, Semantic Web Rule Language is designed on top of ontologies to be an alternative paradigm for the knowledge modeling that adds expressivity to the OWL. Besides this, SWRL rules infer new knowledge from the existing knowledge modeled in the ontologies. SQWRL is the query language of the Semantic Web for querying the RDF data [10]. Along with query language SQWRL, it has more access to characterize on RDF graphs. SWRL rule engine employed with an ontology-based on IFC specifications can be used for the information retrieval process from an IFC model and is the focus of our research.

III. Related Work

To achieve the benefits of ontologies, there are many efforts to build an ontology for the IFC construction industry. One of the outcomes can be seen as an IFC-based Construction Industry Ontology and Semantic Web services framework [11]. With simple reasoning built over the ontology, their information retrieval system could query the IFC model in XML format directly. The BuildingSMART Linked Data Working Group has developed IfcOWL ontology to allow extensions towards other structured data sets that are made available using Semantic Web technologies [12]. There are many versions of IfcOWL ontology since the work has been started. We have been working on an ontology IFC4_ADD1.owl that was launched on 25 Sept. 2015. We have enriched this ontology with English-French and IFC vocabulary (synonyms, descriptions, etc.) from bSDD semantic data dictionary in our research project where we map regulatory text and certification rules over BIM [13]. In addition, we assigned concepts of IfcOWL ontology with Global Unique Identifier (GUID) to serve as a unique language-dependent serial number from the bSDD.

Data models formally define data objects and relationships among data objects for a domain of interest. EXPRESS is a standard data modeling language for product data [25]. There are some research projects that bring BIM to the Web, to overcome drawbacks due to several limitations of EXPRESS, by converting IFC models into RDF graphs. Then, the RDF models become accessible from the Web; they can be processed and queried in more flexible ways, and they can be interlinked using the Linked Data technologies. This way of bringing BIM to the Web allows to take advantage of the fast evolution of the Web and the emerging services and data sources. Hoang and Torma [14] developed an open-source Java based IFC2RDF tool that performs multilayer conversion from IFC schemas developed in EXPRESS into OWL2 ontologies [26] and IFC data from STEP physical file format (SPFF) into RDF graphs aligned with the ontologies. Through the multi-layer model, users can get three ontology layers according to the requirements of an application, where each ontology layer is compatible with essentially the same IFC-derived RDF data. There is another tool named IFC-to-RDF-converter developed by Internet & Data lab at Aalto University and Ghent University [15]. They provide with an EXPRESS-to-OWL and IFC-to-RDF conversion service. The converter can be accessed in a number of ways: using a command line tool (written in Java), using a RESTful Web interface, or using a Graphical User Interface (GUI).

Besides these projects that build an ontology for the IFC, recent years revealed some contributions based on Semantic Web technologies. SWOP-PMO project is one of recent contributions that use formal methodology based on the Semantic Web standards and technologies [16]. It uses OWL/RDF to represent the knowledge, and SPARQL queries and Rule Interchange Format (RIF) to represent the rules. The RDF/OWL representation is not derived from the written knowledge but has to be remodeled in accordance with the rules of OWL/RDF. There are some other works for the semantic enrichment of ontologies in the construction and building domain. Emani et al. proposed a framework for generating an OWL Description Logic (DL) expression of a given concept from its natural language definition automatically [17]. Their framework also takes into account IFC ontology and the resultant DL expression is built by using the existing IFC entities.

Pauwels and Zhang [18] listed three ways for the conformance checking of IFC models. First, we have the hard coded rule checking, which is similar to the approach adopted by Solibri Model Checker [19]. This tool loads a BIM model, considers rules stored natively in the application and performs rule checking against BIM for the architectural design validations. This approach is fast as rules are integrated inside the application, but there is no flexibility or customization possible as rules are not available outside the actual application. Another solution, the traditional approach of compliance checking is with the IfcDoc tool developed by buildingSMART International for generating MVDXML rules through a graphical interface [20]. It is based on the MVDXML specification to improve the consistent and computer-interpretable definition of Model View Definitions as true subsets of the IFC Specification with enhanced definition of concepts. This tool is widely used as AEC specific platform in the construction industry.

The second approach is 'rule checking' by querying the IFC model. In this approach, BIM is interrogated by rules, which are formalized directly into SPARQL queries. As an example, K. R. Bouzidi et al. [21] proposed this approach to ease regulation compliance checking in the construction industry. They reformulated the regulatory requirements written in the natural language via SBVR, and then, SPARQL queries perform the conformance checking of IFC models.

The third is a semantic rule checking approach with dedicated rule languages such as SWRL, Jess [27] or N3Logic [28]. There are few projects in AEC industries that use this approach for the formal rule-checking, job hazard analysis and regulation compliance checking. H. Wicaksono et al. [22] built an intelligent energy management system for the building domain by using RDF representation of a construction model. Then, they formulated SWRL rules to infer anomalies over the ontological model. Later, they also developed SPARQL interface to query the results of rules. Pauwels et al. [23] built acoustic regulation compliance checking for BIM models based on N3Logic rules. They use N3logic rules with an ontology to reason whether a construction model is compliant or not with the European acoustic regulations. Another project that was built on the ontological framework for the rule-based inspection of eeBIM-systems was developed by M. Kadolsky et al. [24]. They used rules to query an IfcOWL ontology that captured a building.

IV. VALIDATION OF CONSTRUCTION MODELS VIA IFCDOC AND SWRL

The validation of IFC building models is vital in the BIM-based collaboration processes. The aim of validating Models is to align several specialized indexations of building components at both sides, assuming that they deal with the same abstract concepts or physical objects, but according to their separate representation prisms. We have adopted two methods for the verification of rules. Firstly, we use IfcDoc tool (MVDXML checker) which performs three step automatic control sequence. The IfcDoc engine loads the IFC file and MVD files, and then executes the defined rules. Finally, it generates a report indicating compliance (compliant/non-compliant) of each item under the rule. It assigns each rule a green or red depending on whether the item is/is-not in compliance to the defined rules. Secondly, we have built a SWRL-based rule engine to verify our rules. For this, we have converted our IFC model into RDF which is the input of the rule engine by using IFC-to-RDF-Converter. Each method has its own pros and cons and should be used according to requirements of the research project. The following subsections present these two approaches of verification, and also present a comparison between two technologies MVDXML and SWRL side by side.

A. *Verify the presence of an Attribute Value*

When we need to access the name/label of an IfcSpace, we can simply access the name attribute of the IFC schema. Figure 1 shows the MVDXML template and Figure 2 illustrates how we can access it with the help of SQWRL. In addition, SQWRL provides a lot of built-in functions which we can apply on the name to get results more appropriate according to their order, size, etc. For example, Figure 2 also illustrates how the names of IfcSpaces are obtained with the help of built-in ordered function (sqwrl:orderBy).

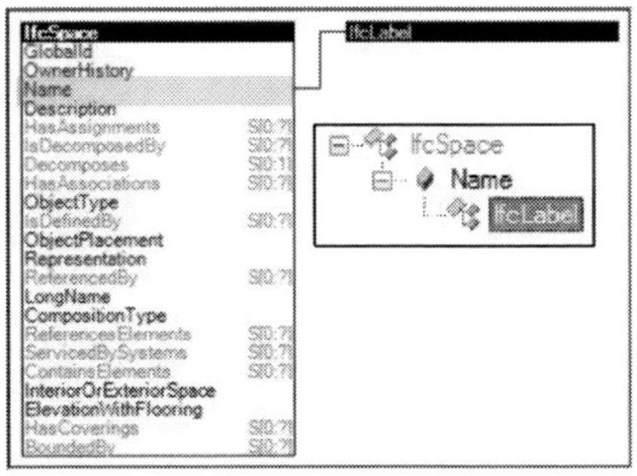

Figure 1. Accessing attribute of IfcSpace in IfcDoc

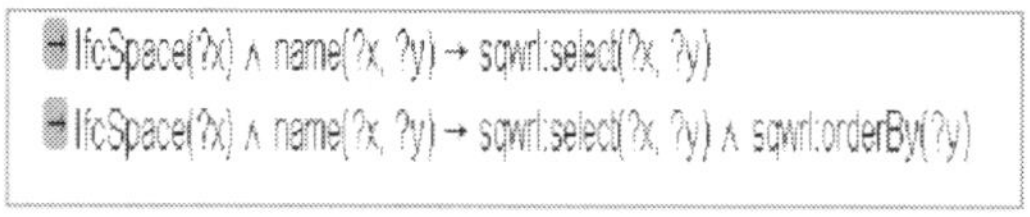

Figure 2. Accessing attribute of IfcSpace in SWRL

B. Verify the presence of an Element

When there is a need to restrict the relation between the elements of IFC, we can use the IfcRelAggregates relation in MVDXML to specify relating objects. For example, Figure 3 illustrates when we want to check IfcProject should contain an IfcBuilding as represented by the cardinality involved between IFC objects. On the other hand, in case of ontology, we can restrict IfcProject by a restriction: IfcProject contains some IfcBuilding, (i.e., IfcProject $\supset \exists$ contains.IfcBuilding) as illustrated in Figure 4. We can also check this with the help of SQWRL by counting the number of buildings related to IfcProject and verifying whether their number is greater than one.

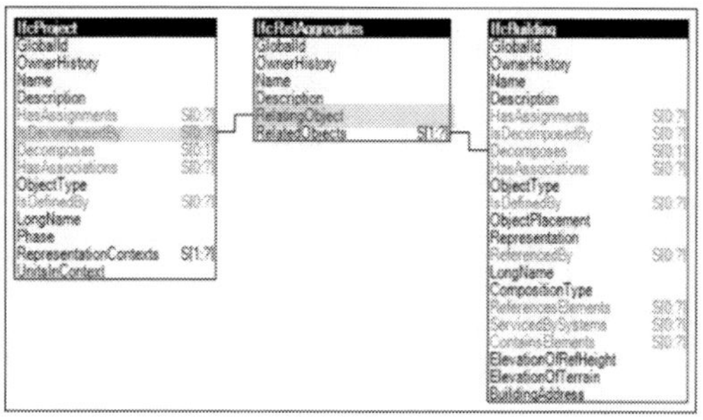

Figure 3. Verify the presence of an element in IfcDoc

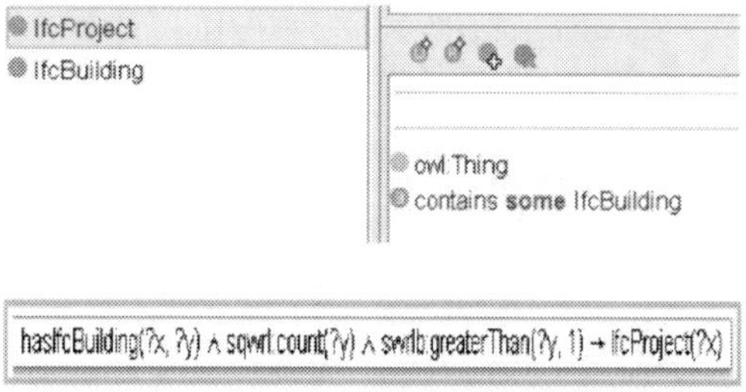

Figure 4. Verify the presence of an element in SWRL

C. Verify the value of a Simple Attribute

In MVDXML and SWRL, we can create various types of conformance checking conditions on the attributes of objects. For example, consider a case when we need to check the value of overAllWidth attribute of a door to be greater than 0.8. Figures 5 and 6 illustrate how we can verify this in these technologies. Both technologies support a lot of operators for the implementation of conditions (such as: $=, \neq, <, >, \leq, \geq$).

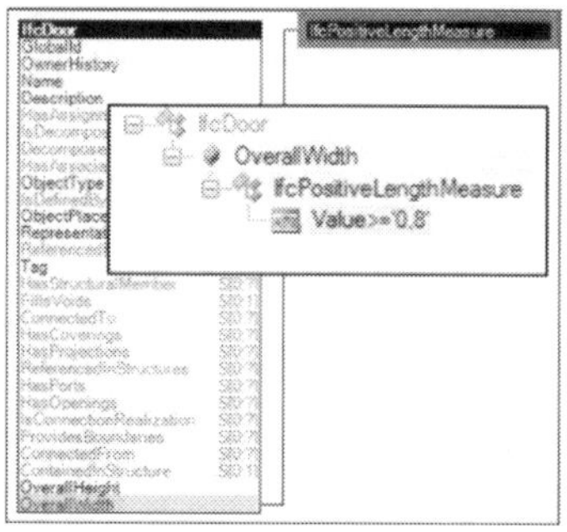

Figure 5. Condition on OverAllWidth attribute of an IfcDoor in IfcDoc

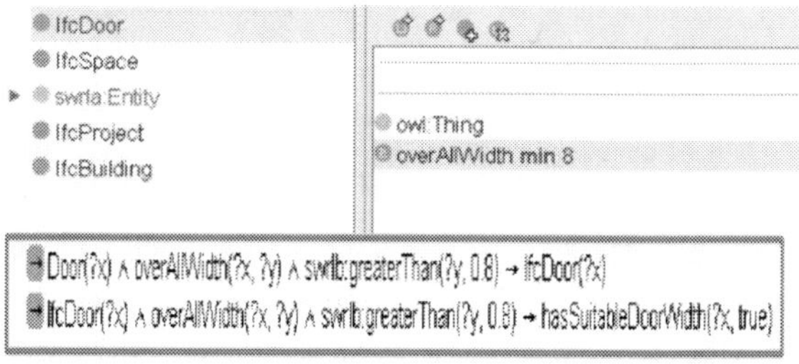

Figure 6. Condition on OverAllWidth attribute of an IfcDoor in SWRL

D. Verify Attributes of Element relative to the Classification

Both technologies allow us to verify attributes of elements relative to the classification. Figures 7a and 7b illustrate how MVDXML and SWRL support various representations of IFC objects with respect to the classifying element.

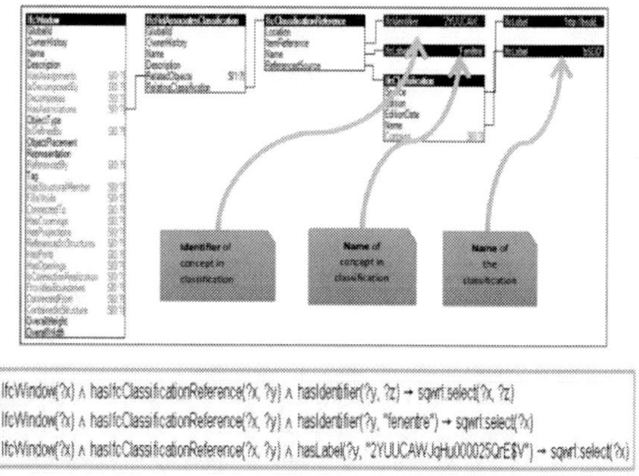

Figure 7. Selection of the concept by 'Fenêtre' in (a) IfcDoc (b) SWRL

E. *Verify the cardinality of an Element*

Both MVDXML and OWL schema allow verifying the cardinality of an element. For an example, they allow to verify whether IfcGroup has two WCs. Figures 8 and 9 illustrate how these technologies support the verification of the cardinality of an element. There can be many ways to perform this semantically, as depicted in the Figure 9.

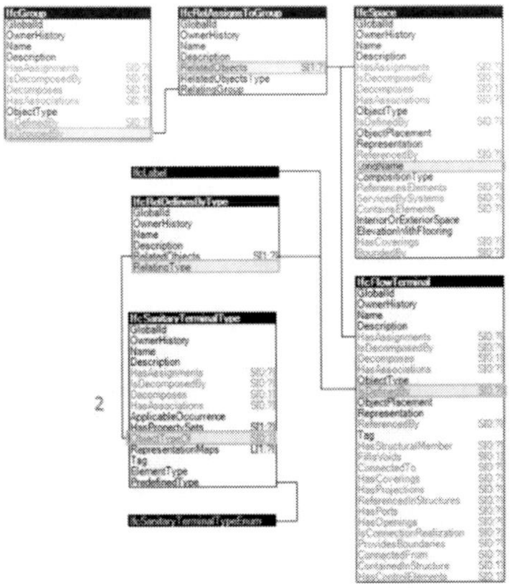

Figure 8. Verifying IfcGroup should have two WC in IfcDoc

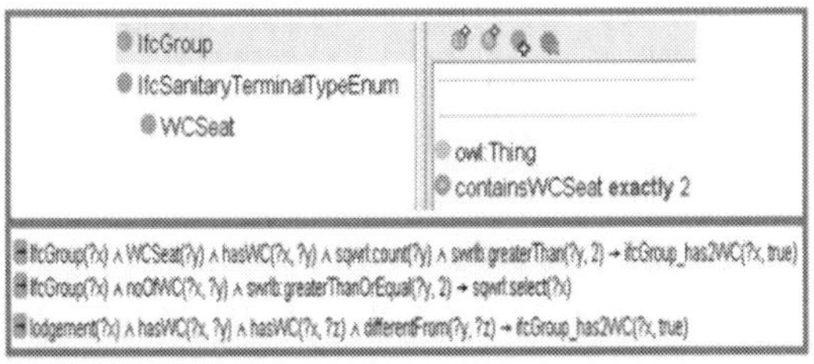

Figure 9. Verifying IfcGroup should have two WC in SWRL

F. *Composition of Simple Rule to build complex rules*

MVDXML and SWRL allow building complex rules which are formed from basic rules. We can concatenate simple rules with operators to form more complex rules. Figures 10 and 11 show an example of building complex rules with the composition of simple rules.

```
<Concept name="Nombre de WC dans le logement">
  <Template ref="1" /><!-- vers le Template : WC séparé-->
  <Template ref="2" /><!-- vers le Template : 2 WC-->
  <TemplateRules operator="and" />
</Concept>
```

Figure 10. Composition of complex rules based on simple rules in IfcDoc

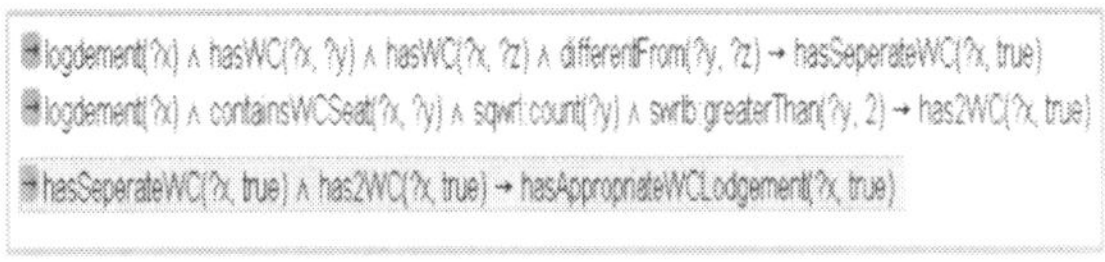

Figure 11. Composition of complex rules based on simple rules in SWRL

G. *Beyond MVDXML – More functionalities in SWRL*

As SWRL is a W3C [29] recommendation, a lot more functionality is added to meet the requirements of the real world scenarios. For example, one can perform calculations in SWRL, which we cannot do in MVDXML. For instance, volume of a door can be calculated given the length, width and height of a door. In SWRL, we use *multiply* function to get *LxWxH* to calculate and display the volume of a door. In addition to a mathematical library (e.g., add, subtract, multiply,..,sin, cos, tan), we have a large number of functions for the string manipulation (e.g., stringConcat, stringLength, substring, normalizeSpace, etc.), and for the DateTime, Duration, URIs and Lists as well. In addition, we can also define new attributes and elements and give them values based on the initial axioms in the repository and store them back in our repository for further processing. This is a very interesting feature of semantic technologies as we cannot define everything in the repository at the initial stage. Some information which is missing, evolving, or new, can be inserted in the repository during the later stages of design and processing. For example, if we want a new attribute isWheelChairAccessible associated with the water closet (WC) based on the dimensions of its door, then we can verify its width and height, and assign a value to the attribute *isWheelChairAccessible* and store its value back in the repository to judge the accessibility of a WC.

V. EXPERIMENTAL ANALYSIS ON IFCDOC AND SPARQL

We also performed experiments via different queries on different sizes of IFC models by the traditional approach via IFCDoc and the ontology-based approach via SPARQL. We have used IFC-to-RDF-Converter developed by Pauwels and Oraskari [15]. The IFC file needs to follow the IFC4_ADD1, IFC4, IFC2X3_TC1, or IFC2X3_Final schema. Once IFC document is converted into RDF, then we stored it into the Stardog triple store. Stardog is the enterprise knowledge graph used for querying, searching, and analyzing enterprise data, wherever it is, using scalable, cutting-edge knowledge graph technology. We found that SPARQL queries are flexible for retrieving data and do the validation in an optimized way giving better run-time as compared to the traditional approach. But conversion from IFC to RDF and then storage of triples into stardog takes time. But, once the stardog triple store is loaded with the data, it is much faster querying and validation of IFC document. SPARQL queries and SWRL rules can be modified easily with the new or customized conditions and constraints for the conformance checking against the stored triple store. Besides flexibility, reasoning is another advantage of Semantic Web technology, as the IfcDoc tool does not provide any justification. With queries and rules, we can identify the reason of inconsistency and anomalies. Therefore, each approach has its own pros and cons. The traditional approach is simpler as there are no conversion tasks. On the other hand, Semantic Web technologies require a conversion layer to be integrated for the validation tasks for IFC models. But, it can enable interoperability and fast information retrieval once the triple store is ready. Table I summarizes file and schema features of both approaches, where 1 represents the traditional approach via MVDXML and 2 represents the Semantic Web approach via SWRL.

TABLE I. FILE AND SCHEMA FEATURES OF BOTH APPROACHES

	Data File	*Rule File*	*Rule Schema*	*Data Schema*
1	IFC	.mvdXML	.XSD	.step
2	RDF (IFC converted)	.SWRL, .OWL	.OWL	IfcOnt

VI. CONCLUSION AND FUTURE WORK

This paper addresses the need of automatic verification requirements to warn the non-conformities with the associated 3D visualization as a hot challenge. We studied two approaches for the validation of IFC Models, i.e., with IfcDoc and SWRL. Each approach has its own pros and cons and should be used according to requirements of a research project. Some of major points are:

- IfcDoc tool and traditional conformance checking by MVDXML technology is a good candidate for the simple rules on small IFC models. Verification by SWRL requires a prior conversion of the IFC model in to the RDF, which is an extra task to achieve.
- Although IFC is an open standard; its complex nature makes information retrieval from an IFC model difficult as the size of IFC model grows. Querying semantic model is faster and gives a good run-time. One can customize queries easily and according to requirements.
- There is no intermediate state and IfcDoc tool gives no explanation for the reason of non-compliance. Whereas the Semantic Web technology is a good compromise between development efforts and opportunities. The graphical representation of RDF allows rules to be more intuitive and more efficient to reason and execute.

As a future direction, we are going to present a comprehensive quantitative comparison between the two approaches, and also investigate other triple stores which are competitors of stardog for the storage and querying of IFC models.

REFERENCES

[1] V. Rebekka, J. Stengel, and F. Schultmann, "Building Information Modeling (BIM) for existing buildings—Literature review and future needs." Automation in construction, vol. 38, pp. 109-127, 2014.

[2] C. Eastman, P. Teicholz, R. Sacks, and K. Liston, "BIM Handbook: A Guide to Building Information Modeling for Owners, Managers, Designers, Engineers, and Contractors", Hoboken, New Jersey, Wiley, 2008.

[3] V. Thein, Industry Foundation Classes (IFC), BIM Interoperability Through a Vendor-Independent File Format, A Bentley White Paper, September 2011.

[4] E. Jönsson, "Consequences of Implementing the buildingSMART Data Dictionary From a construction company's perspective", Stockholm, May 2015.

[5] T. Chipman, T. Liebich, and M. Weise, "mvdXML specification of a standardized format to define and exchange MVD with exchange requirements and validation Rules", version 1.0, May 2012.

[6] T. Mendes de Farias, A. Roxin, and C. Nicolle, "A Semantic Web Approach for defining Building Views", buildingSMART Summit Jeju, Korea, 28 Sept, 2016.

[7] I. Horrocks, P.F. Patel-Schneider, H. Boley, S. Tabet, B. Grosof, and M. Dean, "SWRL: A Semantic Web Rule Language Combining OWL and RuleML", 2004.

[8] SPARQL Query Language for RDF, http://www.w3.org/TR/rdf-sparql-query/, 2008. [last access: June 2017]

[9] Stardog, http://stardog.com/ [last access: June 2017]

[10] D. Brickley, R.V. Guha, and B. McBride, (2004). "RDF vocabulary description language 1.0: RDF Schema". W3C Recommendation 2004. [last access: June 2017]

[11] L. Zhang and R.R. Issa, "Development of IFC-based Construction Industry Ontology for Information Retrieval from IFC Models", International Workshop on Computing in Civil Engineering, Netherlands, Vol. 68, 2011.

[12] W. Terkaj and P. Pauwels, "IfcOWL ontology file for IFC4", 2014. Available at: http://linkedbuildingdata.net/resources/IFC4_ADD1.owl

[13] M. Fahad, Nicolas Bus., and F. Andrieux, "Towards Mapping Certification Rules over BIM", Proc. of the 33rd CIB W78 Conference, Brisbane, Australia, 2016.

[14] N. Vu Hoang, and S. Törmä, "Implementation and Experiments with an IFC-to-Linked Data Converter". Proc. of the 32nd CIB W78 Conference, Netherlands, 2015.

[15] P. Pauwels and J. Oraskari, "IFC-to-RDF Converter" https://github.com/IDLabResearch/IFC-to-RDF-converter

[16] F. Josefiak, H. Bohms, P. Bonsma, and M. Bourdeau, "Semantic product modelling with SWOP's PMO, eWork and eBusiness in AEC", pp. 95-104

[17] C.K. Emani, C. Ferreira Da Silva, B. Fiès, P. Ghodous, and M. Bourdeau., "Automated Semantic Enrichment of Ontologies in the Construction Domain". Proc. of the 32nd CIB W78 Conference, Netherlands, 2015.

[18] P. Pauwels and S. Zhang, "Semantic Rule-Checking for regulation compliance checking: An overview of strategies and approaches". Proc. of the 32nd CIB W78 Conference, Netherlands, 2015.

[19] L. Khemlani, "Solibri model checker", AECbytes Product Review March 31, 2009

[20] IfcDoc Tool, available at: http://www.buildingsmart-tech.org/specifications/ specification-tools /ifcdoc-tool/ifcdoc-help-page-section/IfcDoc.pdf, 2012.

[21] K. R., Bouzidi, B., Fies, C., Faron-Zucker, A. Zarli, and N. Le Thanh, "Semantic Web Approach to Ease Regulation Compliance Checking in Construction Industry". *Future Internet*. 4 (3). pp. 830-851, 2012.

[22] H. Wicaksono, P., Dobreva, P. Häfner, and S. Rogalski, "Ontology development towards expressive and reasoning-enabled building information model for an intelligent

energy management system". Proc. of the 5th KEOD, pp. 38-47. SciTePress, 2013.

[23] P. Pauwels, D. Van Deursen, R. Verstraeten, J. De Roo, R. De Meyer, R. Van de Walle, and J. Van Campenhout, "A semantic rule checking environment for building performance checking". Automation in Construction. 20 (5). pp. 506-518, 2011.

[24] M. Kadolsky, K. Baumgärtel, and R. J. Scherer, An ontology framework for rule-based inspection of eeBIM-systems. Procedia Engineering. vol. 85, pp. 293-301, 2014.

[25] EXPRESS, ISO 10303-11:2004 Industrial automation systems and integration - Product data representation and exchange - Part 11: Description methods: The EXPRESS language reference manual, https://www.iso.org/-standard/38047.html, [last access: June 2017]

[26] OWL 2 Web Ontology Language Document Overview (Second Edition), W3C Recommendation 11 December 2012, https://www.w3.org/TR/owl2-overview/ [last access: June 2017]

[27] E. Friedman-Hill, "Jess in Action: Rule Based Systems in Java". Manning Publications. ISBN 1-930110-89-8, 2003

[28] T. I. M. Berners-Lee, D. A. N. Connolly, L. Kagal, Y. Scharf, and J. I. M. Hendler, "N3Logic: A logical framework for the World Wide Web", Theory and Practice of Logic Programming. vol. 8 (3), 2008.

[29] World Wide Web Consortium (W3C), https://www.w3.org/ [last access: June 2017]

Manipulation of Search Engine Results during the 2016 US Congressional Elections

Panagiotis Takis Metaxas and Yada Pruksachatkun

Department of Computer Science
Wellesley College
Wellesley, MA 02481
Email: pmetaxas@wellesley.edu

***Abstract*—Web spammers are individuals who attempt to manipulate the structure of the Web in such a way that a search engine (SE) will give them higher ranking location (and thus, greater visibility) in search results than what they would get without manipulation. Typically, Web spammers aim to promote their own financial, political or religious agendas exploiting the trust that users associate with SE query results. Over the last ten years, search engines have taken steps to defend against spammers with some success. Arguably, Web spamming is crucial during election times, when voters are likely to use search engines to get information about electoral candidates. At times of elections, spammers could succeed in spreading propaganda manipulating SE query results of candidates' names. In a symmetric but, arguably, less likely scenario, SEs might influence elections by manipulating their own results to favor one candidate over another. In fact, some have suggested that SEs (Google in particular) should be proactively regulated to avoid such a possibility. In this paper, we investigate to what degree the SE query results related to searches of electoral candidates names were altered by anyone (Web spammers or SEs) during the 2016 US congressional election, an election that saw the rise of "fake news" sites. Our results indicate that different SEs had different degree of success defending against spammers: Google gave preference to reliable sources in the first 6 of the top-10 search results when queried with the name of any electoral candidate. Also, Google did not allow much variation in the ranking of the top-10 results and did not allow "fake news" sites to appear at its organic results. Bing and Yahoo, on the other hand, did not have as good a record. This is even more apparent in the autocomplete box "suggest" options presented to the user while forming the query.**

Keywords–Search Engines; US Elections; Web Spam; Fake News; Google; Yahoo; Bing.

I. INTRODUCTION

Web spammers are individuals who are trying to manipulate the structure of the Web in such a way to control search engines ranking algorithms to give them higher ranking in search results than what they would get without the alteration [1]. This way, Web spammed pages will get higher visibility in the eyes of unsuspected users searching for the targeted terms. They do that by manipulating the SE ranking methods aiming to influence the user's opinion about their site's quality. In this respect, they behave very similarly to social propagandists who are trying to alter a citizen's mental trust network in ways beneficial to the propagandist [1].

Web spam has a long history of manipulating search results of SEs that starts with the creation of the first search engine, back in 1995. Usually, their intentions are:

- financial: turning the attention of users to particular products they are promoting, or gaining from online advertisement;
- political: helping elect the candidates they support;
- religious: helping promote the religion they support.

Even though their activities are not known to most Web users, spammers have had a significant role in the evolution of SEs because they have forced SEs to keep changing their ranking methods [2]. Ranking methods, such as the well known PageRank [3] used to be a well-understood, studied and evaluated set of mathematical functions of information retrieval, while today they are a secret, fluid, complicated and intentionally difficult to predict set of factors [4]. Since SE ranking methods is one of the most important factor that any Web site marketer, advertiser, or propagandist needs to understand, there is a whole $65 billion industry that is studying them [5].

A. *Background and Prior Work*

Researchers have followed the election-related Web spamming attempts in the past twelve years or so [6]. The first recorded attempt was in 2006 when spammers openly called for the promotion of negative information related to some candidates for the senate and recorded the results online on the `myDD.com` Web site. However, their initial success draw the attention of Google that reportedly tried to defend against their efforts, since their actions were compromising its reputation as a reliable search engine.

In particular, [7] and [8] studied to what degree Googles electoral search results were manipulated during the six months prior to the 2008 and the 2010 congressional elections. Their findings suggest that starting in 2008, Google tried to protect its search results by reducing the weight that the PageRank algorithm had on searches with queries the names of US electoral candidates. In 2012, Google started employing a vertical split-screen interface in which the left side of the screen contained the organic results and the right side contained information from its *knowledge graph* [9] with official information about the candidate (see Figure 3). Bing and Yahoo have also adopted a similar interface (e.g., see Figures 1 and 2). We should point out that, even though Google's electoral search results has been studied over time, to our knowledge, Bing's and Yahoo's performance to defending against spam has not been studied in depth in the past.

Recently, some researchers have raised the possibility that Google might secretly decide to manipulate its own results

[10]. That is, they worry that Google might be tempted to use its ranking algorithm to support one political candidate over another [11]. In particular, [10] has measured the possible influence that manipulated search results can have on unsuspecting audiences. They have found that, even though the effect of manipulation may not be large, it can have a significant effect in close elections.

While such claims created a lot of interest from news organizations, the realization that people's opinion can be influenced by search results is hardly new. Every advertiser is well aware of the importance of their ranking, and a whole industry, called *"search engine optimization" (SEO)*, has tried to increase product placement through blog posting and even Web spamming. The SEO industry is reportedly worth tens of billions of dollars [5]. SEOs organize conferences and training workshops selling expertise on how one can do exactly this type of manipulation. While the work of [10] is focusing on a particular SE, Google, and has called for federal regulation of its search results, one needs to examine all major SEs for biased behavior. We argue that such a concern is rather overstated: Google is the major SE and it would have everything to lose by manipulating its rankings. Data collection such as the one done for this paper could reveal enough evidence of its manipulation and it could be done by anyone with basic programming skills in scrapping. Further, many people inside Google would know it and the likelihood of a whistleblower is rather high.

Our paper's contributions are as follows: We investigate to what degree the SE query results related to searches of electoral candidates' names showed any signs of alteration by anyone (spammers or SEs) during the six months prior to the 2016 US congressional election. This was an election that saw the rise of "fake news" sites, and so it is doubly important to see to what degree "fake news" stories infiltrated search results. We also examined the number of times that "fake news" sites (that is, sites that have been characterized as hosting "fake news" stories by [12]), appeared in the top-10 search results for the examined SEs.

Our results indicate that the three most commonly used SEs, Google, Yahoo and Bing, had strikingly different degree of success defending against spamming. Google gave consistent preference to reliable and official sources in the top-6 search results when queried with the name of any electoral candidate, and did not allow much variation in the ranking of the top-10 results. Bing and Yahoo, on the other hand, do not have as good a record. Their search results showed little effort of consistency and the number of "fake news" sites appearing in their results were higher. This was especially obvious in the search autocomplete box "suggest" options presented to the user forming the query.

The rest of the paper is organized as follows: The next Section II describes our data collection and preparation for analysis, Section III explains our methods, while Section IV describes our results. Finally, Section V contains our conclusion and future work.

II. Data Collection and Preparation

According to the Pew Foundation [13], Google, Bing and Yahoo have a combined market share of 98.34% with the greater portion going to Google (79.88%). It is safe to assume that if there was a successful attempt to manipulate SE results before the US elections, one could detect its success by monitoring the query results for suspicious variations during that period in these three SEs.

For the six months prior to the November 2016 US presidential and congressional elections, we collected query results using as query strings the names of the two major presidential candidates Donald Trump and Hillary Clinton, for Bernie Sanders (because at the beginning of the data collection he was still a contestant for the Democratic nomination) and of 340 congressional candidates, 150 of them Republican, 142 of them Democratic, and 64 of them of smaller parties or unaffiliated (58 independent or libertarian, and 6 local parties). Of these candidates, 74 were running for the 34 seats in the Senate, so we examined every senatorial candidate. We also examined 279 candidates for the House. The latter were a subset of the more than 2000 candidates running for the 435 seats in the House. To avoid overloading the SEs with over 2000 query requests, we selected the candidates for the first six states, in alphabetical order: AL, AK, AZ, AR, CA, CO. We have no reason to believe that the search results in the remaining states would have been any different. The candidate names were chosen from a website specializing in monitoring the electoral candidates [14].

We used the following method to collect the data: between June 2 and November 8, 2016, on a roughly bi-weekly basis (44 data collection dates in total), Google, Bing, and Yahoo were queried and scraped for the top 10 results using `requests` and `urllib` python libraries, and matching using regular expressions for the top 10 results tags. Each of the search results were then aggregated into files for each candidate, as follows: for each collection date, each candidates file contains a list of websites that appeared in the top 10 search results, in the numerical order they appeared. For consistency in the overall data collection, websites that did not appear in the top-10 results for a certain date were assigned a rank of 0 for that date.

We point out an caveat in our data collection. In the middle of the search results scraping, Bing changed its formatting a couple of times (at least) and our algorithms collected fewer top-10 results in a consistent fashion. The analysis we present here is based on the earlier dates and may be incorrect for Bing overall.

III. Method and Analysis

Processing the data involved the following steps: for each candidate, we created a table with the top-10 links per date for each of the 44 data collection dates. We wanted to know the particular domain that a link was pointing to, instead of the specific link within the site. To account for that, we extracted the site domain of each link. For example, all articles from the New York Times were represented in our data tables by the site domain `nytimes.com`.

For each domain in the table, we calculated the number of times it appeared over the whole collection period. To control for data sparsity, we introduced the measure of *website appearance percentage* (WAP), defined as the minimum percentage of times a website appeared in the top-10 results over the period of data collection. For the data reported below, we used WAP values of 33%, 50%, 66% and 75%.

We also compute a domain's *mode*, defined as the top-10 location it appeared for a WAP percentage of the time.

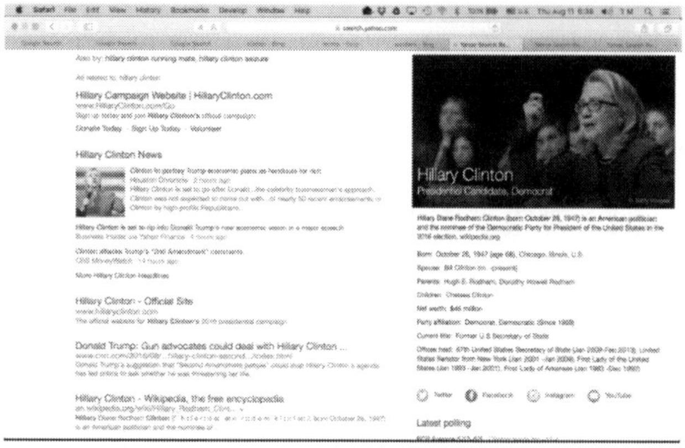

Figure 1. Yahoo sample search results for Hillary Clinton on Aug. 11, 2016. The first item is an ad, followed by recent news. Organic results start with her official site, cnn and wikipedia. The knowledge graph's information appears on the RHS.

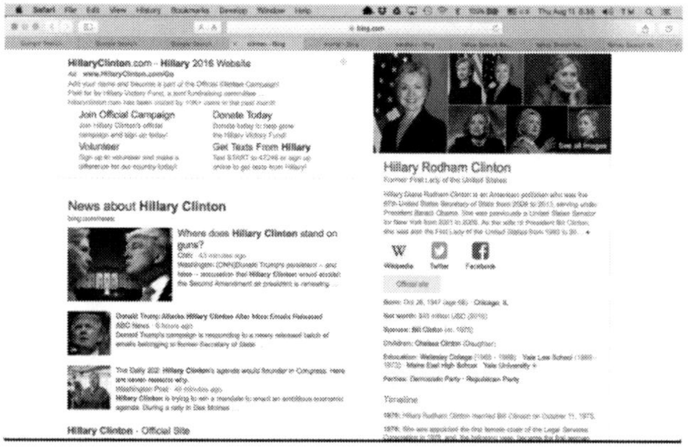

Figure 2. Bing sample search results for Hillary Clinton on Aug. 11, 2016.

For less than a particular WAP, the mode is not defined. One way to get a sense of the usefulness of defining the mode is to think in terms of predicting future search results for some query. Consider the following example: In Google's complete collection for "Hillary Clinton" the URL item `hillaryclinton.com`, her official campaign site, had a mode of 1 with a WAP of 0.75. That means that, at least 75% of the time, searching for "Hillary Clinton" on Google resulted in her official campaign page being first in the top 10 results. It also means that next time we could do the same search, at least 3 out of 4 chances is that `hillaryclinton.com` will appear in the 1st position. Similarly, for the same search, `wikipedia.com`'s mode was 2 and `twitter.com` was 3.

In summary, the higher the WAP we could define for the modes of domains of search results, the more predictable the ranking of search results will be in a future search, and the less likely the search results were altered by propagandists of the SE itself.

IV. RESULTS

Given the plethora of news, blogs and political analysis around the time of elections, if SEs was using a dynamic ranking method, such as straightforward PageRank, to compute

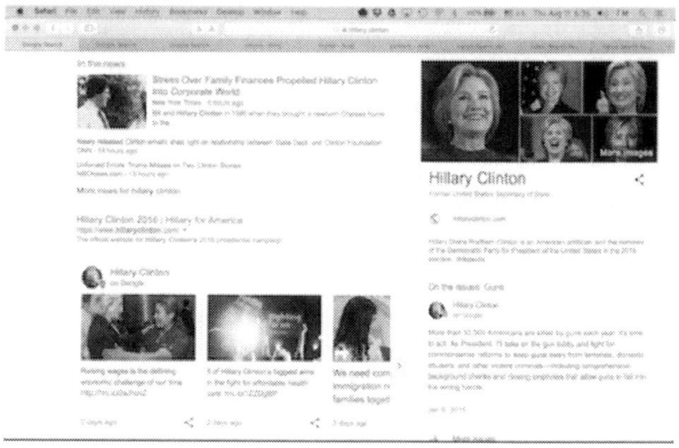

Figure 3. Google sample search results for Hillary Clinton on Aug. 11, 2016. Note that all three SEs have adopted the "knowledge graph" on the RHS of each search, which makes them even more visible occupying a large portion "above the fold". For prominent candidates, the LHS may contain an ad followed by recent news about the candidate. Our research measures the changes in the "organic results" typically appearing under news.

the top-10 results, it would be surprising to have mode defined at all. It is more reasonable to think that, as news was being produced and gaining prominence in online sources, the location of every URL item would change considerably over time. On the other end, if SEs were using a static list of predefined top-10 results to respond to search queries, all 10 modes would be defined over the data collection.

Of course PageRank is one of the factors that search engines are using to rank their results. The greater the contribution of PageRank in the final ranking, the less often mode is defined. Intuitively, when for a search query we have a large number of modes defined, say 6–10 modes per candidate collection, we can deduce that the query results are not updated dynamically over time as much. But if a small number of modes were defined, say 0-4 modes, the query results are rather dynamically altered, possibly driven by PageRank or spammers. Finally, when 5 modes are only defined, one would say that dynamic and static ranking methods are equally at work.

In any case, we should also point out that it is important to consider *which* modes are defined. For example, if all modes at the top-5 locations are defined, the user will be shown practically the same results above the fold. For users who do not look below the fold, it would appear that search results are not changing.

To see the significance of the number of modes defined in some search result, consider the following scenario. Assume that for some search engine, query results over time for some candidate define 8 modes. That means that, since ranking does not change a lot, the next time we are querying the search engine for the candidate we may expect to see the same 8 URLs in the same location of the search results. So, we can say that we can predict most of the search results. In particular, it is very likely that the above-fold search results (often referred as the top-5) will be the substantially same in the future.

Let us compare that scenario with another scenario of a search engine or candidate whose search defines only 3 modes. In this case, the search result URLs will be significantly different. If Web spammers are trying to influence the search results this latter search engine could fall victim. To be fair, if the 3 modes defined are the top-3, it would indicate an attempt by a search engine to defend its search results in the locations above the fold that are more important, while leaving the rest to the algorithm.

Our mode of location results for our data collections are as follows:

1) Google mode averages for different WAPs:

WAP	75%	66%	50%	33%
Overall	5.37	5.78	6.64	7.50
Democrats	5.32	5.78	6.66	7.67
Republicans	5.44	5.83	6.67	7.45
Senate	5.18	5.55	6.54	7.38
House	5.43	5.85	6.69	7.56

2) Yahoo mode averages for different WAPs:

WAP	75%	66%	50%	33%
Overall	2.67	2.92	3.28	3.21
Democrats	2.57	2.85	3.17	3.13
Republicans	2.75	2.93	3.35	3.26
Senate	2.68	2.93	3.31	3.18
House	2.65	2.89	3.26	3.19

3) Bing mode averages for different WAPs: As we mentioned, due to problems with scraping Bing our results are not complete and so we will not present them here. For the period we have complete results we can report that Bing's mode averages are even lower than Yahoo's.

Our results indicate remarkably different number of modes (and therefore, ranking methods) between Google and the other search engines, even for the more restrictive WAP of 75%. For Google, it is possible to define the mode of each Google search for an average of 5.37 top-10 locations (median = 6) in all of our 340 searches. For WAP 50% (i.e., at least half the time) almost 7 modes are defines (6.64 to be exact). On the other hand, in Yahoo, it is only possible to define the mode for an average of 2.67 locations (median = 3) for WAP 75% and 3.28 for WAP 50%. Finally, in Bing it appears that the average is even less than Yahoo's. In other words, users who queried Google about a congressional candidate, they saw little variation above-fold in their organic search results over time. Users who queried Yahoo saw much greater variation but not in the first 3 organic locations, while users who used Bing saw almost always different results, except maybe in the first location.

But which modes are defined? Not surprising, for all SEs, the most common predicted modes were the top results, with Bing's being the top 2, Google's being the top 7, and Yahoo's being the top 5. This shows that Google contains more websites that are consistently appearing in the top-10 results than Yahoo and Bing.

If spammers (or the search engines themselves) were trying to manipulate their congressional search results, they were not succeeding in Google. It is much more likely that they were successful in Yahoo and, especially in Bing.

Next, we will address the question whether search engines showed any preference to a particular party. Were there any differences in the modes for Democratic and Republican candidates?

The answer is no, all three SEs treated the candidates of both parties in a similar way: Compared to the overall average of 6.64 (for WAP = 50%), Google's mode of Democratic candidates was 6.66 while for Republicans was 6.67. Similarly for Yahoo (3.17 and 3.35, respectively) and Bing.

Remarkably, the averages for Senate candidates vs. House candidates are similarly consistent. Google's Senatorial candidates have average of 6.54 and House candidates 6.69. Yahoo's averages are 3.31 and 3.26, respectively.

Thus, while Google showed little alteration to its organic search results compared to Yahoo and Bing, all three search engines treated all candidate, Democratic or Republican, for Senate or for House, consistently.

A. *"Fake news" stories*

Finally, we counted the occurrences of items from sites that were characterized as "fake news" sites appearing in [12]. We discovered that over all SEs and over all the searches, there were 85 "fake news" sites in Democratic candidate search results, 139 for Republicans, and 27 for independents. Thus, there are more appearances of "fake news" sites in search results of Republican candidates. We should clarify that we have done no analysis as of this writing on whether the "fake news" items were positive or negative for the candidate, or whether the stories were true or false. Doing so is beyond the scope of this paper.

We then counted the number of "fake news" occurrences per search engine. For Google, there were 68 unique stories from sites characterized as "fake news" sites that appeared over the six months period we studied. By contrast, there were 83 for Bing, and 95 for Yahoo. Thus, Google is less prone to listing "fake news" sites in its top-10 results, followed by Bing and last Yahoo. Again, we should clarify that we have done no analysis as of this writing to see whether the "fake news" items appearing on top-10 results were true or false (given that not every story that appears in a "fake news" site may be false).

V. CONCLUSIONS

Our paper studied the extent to which Google, Bing, and Yahoo were prone to Web spamming during the last 2016 congressional elections. While we cannot be sure whether anyone tried to manipulate search results ranking for congressional candidates, we can tell whether they were successful in altering the ranking of the search results, if they tried.

Our results indicate that, by and large, there were no variations of top-6 websites in Google, and only a few "fake news" stories that appeared over the six months period we studied in the top-10 results. On the other hand, there was significant variation in the search results for Yahoo and almost constant change in Bing. If spammers were trying to manipulate search results in Yahoo and Bing, they were more successful. We also found that all three search engines treated similarly Democratic and Republican candidates, and Senatorial and House candidates.

Even though the market share for Yahoo and Bing is small, spammers can introduce biased information into the search results, affecting the perception of candidates for users who used these two SEs. Further evidence of the ease at which Bing and Yahoo are manipulated by spammers can be found [15]. Thus, we call for a thorough effort by Bing and Yahoo to increase their defense against Web spammers. Further investigations are needed for Yahoo and Bing data, as well as for the nature and type of any spam that were introduced to various demographics of candidates.

References

[1] C. Castillo and B. Davison, *Adversarial Web Search*, ser. Foundation and trends in information and technology. Now Publishers, 2011. [Online]. Available: http://bit.ly/2pdYxrZ

[2] P. Metaxas, "Web Spam, Social Propaganda and the Evolution of Search Engine Rankings," *Lecture Notes BIP, Springer-Verlag*, 2010. [Online]. Available: http://bit.ly/ffYsuC

[3] L. Page, S. Brin, R. Motwani, and T. Winograd, "The pagerank citation ranking: Bringing order to the web." Stanford InfoLab, Technical Report 1999-66, November 1999, previous number = SIDL-WP-1999-0120. [Online]. Available: http://ilpubs.stanford.edu:8090/422/

[4] "Google Keeps Tweaking Its Search Engine," 2007, URL: http://nyti.ms/2n5JjGx [accessed: 2007-06-03].

[5] "The SEO industry is worth $65 billion; will it ever stop growing?" 2016, URL: http://selnd.com/2p0PyvV [accessed: 2017-02-01].

[6] "Propaganda, Misinformation, "Fake News", and what to do about it." 2017, URL: http://bit.ly/2qQkwpn [accessed: 2017-05-11].

[7] P. Metaxas, "Network Manipulation (with application to political issues)," in *Proceedings of the Interdisciplinary Workshop on Information and Decision in Social Networks, Cambridge, MA, May 31 - June 1, 2011*. MIT Media Lab, May 2011, URL: http://bit.ly/NRmNox/ [accessed: 2017-02-15].

[8] P. T. Metaxas and E. Mustafaraj, "The battle for the 2008 us congressional elections on the web," in *In the Proceedings of the 2009 WebScience: Society On-Line Conference*, March 2009.

[9] "Knowledge Graph – Inside Search – Google." 2017, URL: http://bit.ly/2r9QOvG [accessed: 2017-05-11].

[10] R. Epstein and R. E. Robertson, "The search engine manipulation effect (SEME) and its possible impact on the outcomes of elections," *PNAS*, pp. E4512–E4521, 2015.

[11] "Could Google rankings skew an election? New group aims to find out." 2017, URL: http://wapo.st/2r7WSFg [accessed: 2017-05-11].

[12] "List of False, Misleading, Clickbait-y, and/or Satirical "News" Sources," 2016, URL: http://bit.ly/2pe1ZmC [accessed: 2017-01-02].

[13] "Search engine use over time," 2012, URL: http://pewrsr.ch/2q2htgx [accessed: 2016-02-15].

[14] "2016 US Congressional Elections Candidates," 2016, URL: http://www.politics1.com/p2016.htm [accessed: 2016-06-02].

[15] "Dr. Epstein, You Dont Understand How Search Engines Work." 2017, URL: http://bit.ly/2pE2Ifl [accessed: 2017-05-11].

Measuring Heart Rate with Mobile Devices for Personal Health Monitoring

Toon De Pessemier and Luc Martens

imec - WAVES - Ghent University
Technologiepark-Zwijnaarde 15
9052 Ghent, Belgium
Email: toon.depessemier@ugent.be luc1.martens@ugent.be

Abstract—**The growing availability of mobile devices, such as smartphones, fitness trackers, and smart watches, induce an increased interest in personal health monitoring. These devices are equipped with the necessary sensor hardware, such as accelerometer and heart rate sensor, for measuring physical activities and heartbeat. However, the accuracy of these measurements is still unclear. In this paper, we evaluate heart rate monitoring with four different device types: a specialized device with a chest strap, a fitness tracker, a smart watch, and a smartphone using plethysmography. The results show similar measurements for the four devices in a state of rest. In contrast, during physical activities the fitness tracker, smart watch, and smartphone may register sudden variations in heart rate with a delay, due to physical movements of the wrist or hand. The specialized device with chest strap shows the most accurate heart rate, highly correlated with measurements obtained with a blood pressure monitor that is approved for medical purposes. These results are important for developers who use data of heart rate for mobile applications and services.**

Keywords*–*Wearable computers; Health information management.

I. Introduction

Obesity and insufficient physical activity are an ever growing problem in modern society. Obesity can induce amongst others, heart diseases and stroke, diabetes, gallbladder disease, and gallstones. Research has shown that the majority of health care costs [1] are due to physical inactivity [2]. Recent research in health care supports the theory that regular physical activity and a healthy diet are much more effective than traditional medication to cure diabetes [3]. Nutrition and training schedules can be downloaded from the Internet, but are often inadequate for users' personal needs or physical capacities and static without taking into account users' progress.

Therefore, new efforts are made to decrease national obesity levels [4], thereby using technology, such as multi-modal sensors, web frameworks, and data mining. Multi-modal sensors enable real-time monitoring of physical activities, such as exercises performed by the user. In the domain of public health monitoring, most applications of these sensors keep track of energy expenditure while performing daily activity [5][6]. The resulting data can be used in a lifestyle recommender that encourages users to adopt a more healthy way of life. With the evolution of Web 2.0 [7], more formal and informal health information has become available, with the perspective of a new generation of well-informed, healthy individuals. This phenomenon is often referred to as *eHealth 2.0*. eHealth 2.0 turns users into health information producers and consumers by offering a multitude of health information data [8][9].

To cope with the problem of information overload incurred by Web 2.0 and its eHealth 2.0 counterpart, recommender systems are used as an effective information filter and at the same time as a tool for providing personal advice through suggestions [10][11]. Recommender systems can e.g. suggest a specific fitness activity or a running trail out of the many available physical activities. Suggestions for physical activities should be tailored to the physical capabilities of each individual. Measuring the physical activity of a person through sensors, such as accelerometers, is insufficient to estimate that person's physical capabilities. Heart rate measurements combined with motion sensors can be used to assess the intensity of physical activities for a person and his/her physical limits [12].

Although specialized devices exist for measuring heart rate, most people do not have these at their disposal. Nowadays, popular mobile devices and wearables are equipped with sensors that promise to measure heart rate as well. However, the accuracy of these heart rate measurements is still unclear. Manufacturers choose not to assert claims regarding the accuracy of the detection of (abnormal) beating patterns; otherwise their gadget would get classified as a medical device and would have to undergo FDA (Food and Drug Administration) regulatory scrutiny [13]. Therefore, the research question of this paper is: how accurate are heart rate measurements of these devices for physical activities with different intensity? This is investigated by an application (developed on Android for this research) for monitoring heart rate of test subjects simultaneously with different devices, during various physical activities. These results are important for all (mobile) applications and services that rely on heart rate data from these devices.

The remainder of this paper is structured as follows. Section II gives an overview of related work in the domain of eHealth and mobile health apps. Section III discusses existing methods for heart rate measuring. The various types of mobile devices for heart rate measuring are listed in Section IV. In Section V, details about our measuring method and our experiences with the various devices are discussed. The results of the measurement experiments are provided in Section VI. In Section VII, conclusions are drawn and future work is mentioned.

II. Related Work

The domain of eHealth has been evolved by two major influences: on the one hand by the increasing availability of sensors for tracking physical activities, not only in smartphones but also in other devices, such as smart wearables; on the other hand by the easy accessibility of health information, stimulating the users' interest for monitoring their physical condition. This evolution has brought the problem of information overload [14] to the healthcare sector. For example, too many diet plans and sport schedules are available, but only a minority are tailored to the specific needs of a person. This emphasizes the need to personalize the health information, which is ongoing since the mid-90s [15] and is demonstrated in Computer-Tailoring Health Education Systems [14].

Personalization can be achieved by a recommender system. Personalized recommendations, customized information, and tailored messages have shown to be far more effective than the non-personalized alternative [11][16]. Health promotion and wellness driven applications often use collaborative filtering techniques to cope with the overload of health info and identify the most relevant data [17]. The selection is not made by a central agency or individual, but based on actions of the community. As a result, the quality of the selection is depending on the size and engagement of the community.

Various Health Information Systems (HIS) have been proposed in recent years. These HIS may have three primary goals: inform, assist in the decision making, or convince the end-user. In the HOMEY project, technology for innovative tele-medicine services is developed [18]. The goal of these services is to effectively manage an incremental dialogue between a tele-medicine system and a patient, taking into account user needs, preferences, and the time course of her/his disease. More specifically, the focus was on an automated, telephone-based home monitoring service for chronic hypertensive patients [19]. Patients are regularly asked to specify their blood pressure values and heart rate. Based on these data, suggestions for physical activities are provided e.g., "Are you still swimming two times a week?" or health advice is offered, such as "You should stop smoking". The personalized dialog with the patient is based on goals and rules specified by medical staff. A clinical trial involving 300 hypertensive patients showed a blood pressure decrease in the group of patients exploiting the Homey service. This study emphasizes the importance of the usability of the HIS to stimulate an intensive use. In contrast to our Android application, the Homey service is not able to automatically measure heart rate.

On the mobile platform, tens of thousands health apps are available [20], often called mHealth (Mobile Health) apps [21]. Sometimes, the offer of health apps is even considered as an overload for medical professionals and consumers [22]. Both continue to express concerns about the quality of many apps [20]. Moreover, the importance of personalization strengthens the need to automatically acquire personal data, such as performed physical activities or heart rate.

However, tracking physical activities or measuring heart rate is complex and maybe insufficiently accurate with general-purpose wearables. For commercially available breast belt measuring devices, evaluations in terms of accuracy have been performed [23]. However for newer wearable devices, the actual accuracy is still unclear. A limited number of studies investigated the accuracy of heart rate monitoring using wearable devices. Heart rate monitoring using a wrist-worn personal fitness tracker has been investigated in non-moving conditions (with patients in the intensive care unit) [24]. The heart rate values obtained using the personal fitness tracker were slightly lower than those derived from continuous electrocardiographic monitoring. The authors argued that further evaluation is required to see if personal fitness trackers can be used in hospitals, e.g. as early warning systems. Another study has investigated the accuracy of step counts and heart rate monitoring with wearables [25]. Test subjects were asked to walk a number of steps during the measurements. The accuracy of the heart rate measurements with the tested wearable devices showed to be very high. In contrast, our paper investigates the accuracy of heart rate monitoring during intense physical activities and with various types of wearable devices.

III. Measuring Heart Rate

Various methods to measure heart rate exist. Two important methods will be discussed in more detail: electrocardiography and photoplethysmography. Others are echocardiography, and measurements based on carotid pulse or radial pulse.

A. *Electrocardiography (ECG)*

Electrocardiography is the process of recording the electrical activity of the heart using electrodes placed on the skin [26]. These electrodes detect the tiny electrical changes on the skin that arise from the heart muscle's electrophysiologic pattern of depolarizing during each heartbeat. In professional environments, such as hospitals, this technique is applied with 10 electrodes, placed on the patient's limbs and on the surface of the chest. The signals of the various electrodes are combined into an electrocardiogram [27], a record of the electrical activity of the heart over a period of time.

B. *Photoplethysmography (PPG)*

Photoplethysmography is the scientific name of Optical Heart rate Sensing (OHS). It is a technique to monitor heart rate based on the combination of photo diodes and LEDs [28]. Blood absorbs green light (hence its red color). As a result, the photo diode detects a reduction in green light intensity during a pulse of the heart. A low intensity of the green light corresponds to a pulse; a high intensity is measured during periods between two pulses. A green LED provides the most accurate results. However, an infrared LED is often used since this consumes less energy. A disadvantage of this method is that motion artifacts have been shown to be a limiting factor. This hinders accurate readings during exercise and free living conditions. In addition, person-dependent variations may also cause distorted readings. For example, a different blood perfusion induces a different absorption of light, thereby registering a deviated reading.

Since the hardware of a smartphone camera is very similar to a pulse-oximeter, it can be used for measuring heart rate by PPG. This works as follows. The index finger is covering the camera lens and the LED. The light from the LED is reflected by the skin of the finger through diffusion; then this light is captured by the camera lens. Contrary to traditional OHS, the red spectrum is often used on smartphones, because the device-specific distribution of red pixels varies less than the distribution of green pixels. Still, this technique relies on hardware-dependent parameters, such as the number of pixels, the LED, etc.

IV. Measuring Devices

Four types of devices for measuring heart rate can be distinguished.

A. Specialized devices

The main purpose of this type of devices is measuring. Therefore, these devices often have only a limited number of sensors and a limited number of features. Examples are heart rate chest straps, pulse-oximeters, and blood pressure monitors. These devices are often approved for medical use and can therefore be used as reference devices.

In this study, the Polar H7 was used. This is a popular heart rate chest strap, which produces very accurate readings (correlation of 0.97 with true heart rate [29]). To test its accuracy, we compared the measurements of the Polar H7 to the ones of the Omrom M6 Comfort [30]. The Omrom M6 is a blood pressure monitor that is approved for medical purposes, and can therefore be considered as the correct heart rate.

The measurements with two users, at two different times, showed that the Polar device produces heart rate measurements with a precision similar to the Omrom. This justifies the use of the Polar H7 as specialized device for heart rate monitoring. Since a blood pressure monitor is rather expensive and less suitable for sports activities, we chose the Polar H7 as reference device during our experiments.

B. Fitness trackers / fitness wearables

These devices, typically worn around the wrist, measure motion, such as counting up steps, monitoring sleep, and calculating the difference between a light jog and a mad sprint. These devices are packed with multiple sensors, such as a 3-axis accelerometer to track movement in every direction, and an altimeter that can measure your altitude, handy for tracking the height of the mountains you have climbed. Some come with a gyroscope too, to measure orientation and rotation. These devices are often not approved for medical purposes, but are cheaper than the specialized devices. The Microsoft Band 2 was chosen for this study because of two reasons. It allows the real time analysis of sensor data and Microsoft provides a comprehensive API. This API allows for example to aggregate the results of a query thereby shifting the computational load to the Microsoft servers.

C. Smart wearables / watches

Similar to fitness trackers, smart wearables and smart watches are equipped with various sensors and are not medically approved. In contrast, fitness trackers their main focus is on tracking physical activities, whereas the goal of smart wearables is more general including tracking physical activities, context recognition, and informing users. The target group of these devices contains not only sports people but also a broader group of people who like the design, or the extra features of a smart watch. Compared to fitness trackers, smart wearables often have more hardware capabilities (e.g., color screen, more processing power), allowing to extend their functionality with additional apps. In this study, the Huawei Watch is used because of its popularity and typical smart watch functionality. To capture heart rate data in real time from the Huawei Watch, a special Wear app was developed. The Wear app communicates with our Android app running on a smartphone through the Wearable Data Layer API.

D. Secondary device feature

This category covers hardware components of devices that allow measuring heart rate. By using (hardware-specific) apps, smartphones are able to measure heart rate using the built-in camera and LED flash based on PPG techniques. In this study, the camera and LED of the Google Nexus 6P are used.

V. MEASUREMENT METHOD

Heart rate measurements are collected and stored on a smartphone (Google Nexus 6P) by a self-developed Android app, since most wearables have a direct bluetooth communication channel. For every device, a service was running on the smartphone to transfer the raw sensor data to the smartphone.

Since different sensors are differently calibrated, differences in the measurements can be witnessed for the same person in the same conditions. Therefore, the heart rate data is normalized based on three levels: resting, walking at low ($\leq$ 4m/s) speed, and walking at high speed. This normalization method has shown its usefulness for physical activities of different intensities [31][32]. This normalization is performed as follows. For each of the activity levels, the heart rate is measured using the different devices simultaneously and over a long period of time ($>$ 10 minutes). For each of the devices, the difference in average heart rate with the reference device (Omrom M6) is calculated. This difference is compensated in the measurements during physical activities (Figure 1, 2, 3, and 4). First, we discuss our practical experiences with the four devices used for measurements.

A. Specialized device: sensor with chest strap

This device is comfortable during sports, while holding its position on the chest. After all, this kind of devices is designed for measuring heart rate during sports.

B. Fitness tracker

Although the Microsoft Band 2 is a fitness tracker designed for sports, we do not experience it as ideal for heart rate measurements from a practical viewpoint. The device hinders when the wrist moves during exercises.

C. Smart watch

During the experiment, we witnessed that motions of the wrist disturb the measurements, even if the strap is tightened excessively. The sensor in the smart watch loses the reference point and measuring the heart rate is interrupted. To cope with this problem, our developed app starts to recalibrate as soon as the measuring process is interrupted. Also variations in light intensity showed to disturb the measurement process. If the wrist is moved to a position where it absorbs more light, measurements turned out to be invalid.

D. Secondary device feature: PPG on smartphone

Using the PPG technique on a smartphone to measure heart rate also has some practical difficulties. The PPG technique is influenced by personal characteristics of the (blood / finger of the) test user. In addition, PPG is very sensitive to motion; so the user has to keep his/her finger still on the flash LED. This complicates heart rate measurements during physical activities. Moreover, the prolonged use of the flash LED and camera heats up the phone excessively. The device becomes so hot, making it impossible to put your finger in the correct position on the LED for a long time. The heating of the device is associated with a drain of the battery. In our experiments, we witnessed a 4% decrease of the battery level during each measurement of 5 minutes.

VI. MEASUREMENT RESULTS

Table I shows the resulting heart rate measurements for two test subjects in rest condition (home environment) without normalization. PPG using a camera is not included, since this method is highly influenced by the type of smartphone that is used. The first user (TS1 - female) has a high heart rate, whereas the other test subject (TS2 - male) has a low heart rate in rest condition. Measurements are repeated at two different times for the two persons. For each device, the average, standard deviation, and median are listed in Table I. The results show that all devices provide consistent results. So in rest conditions, heart rate measurements of these devices can be considered as reliable. The measurements of the Polar H7 are the most similar to the measurements of the Omrom M6, which can be considered as the correct heart rate.

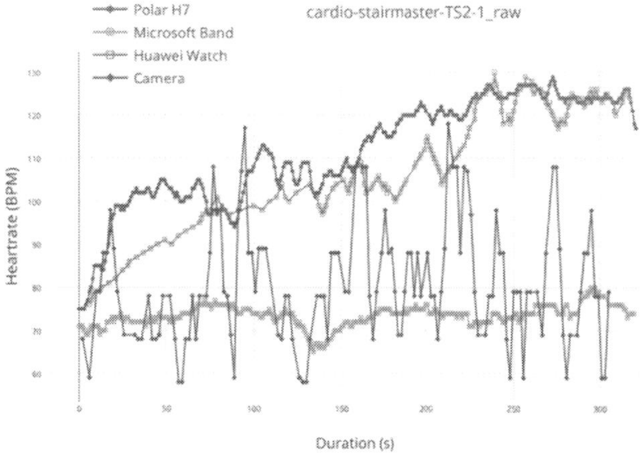

Figure 1. Heart rate measured during stair master.

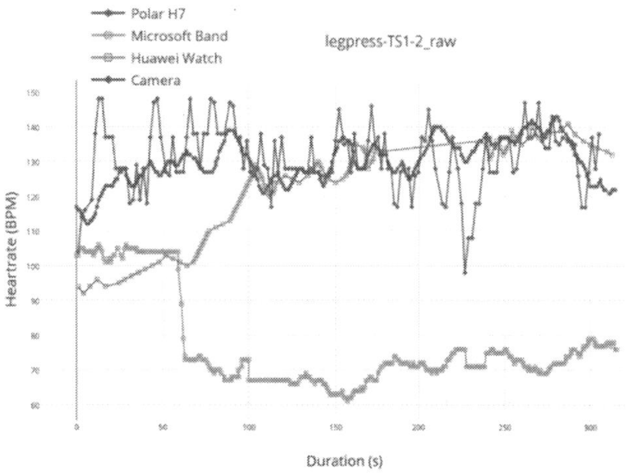

Figure 2. Heart rate measured during leg press.

Figure 1, 2, 3, and 4 show the heart rate measurements obtained with the four devices for four different exercises, respectively Stair Master, Leg Press, Dumbbell Curl, and Long Walking. All exercises are performed in a fitness room by two persons with similar results. The results of one person

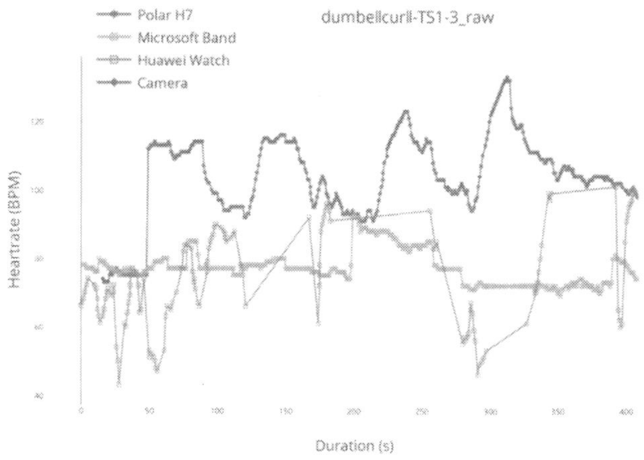

Figure 3. Heart rate measured during dumbbell curl.

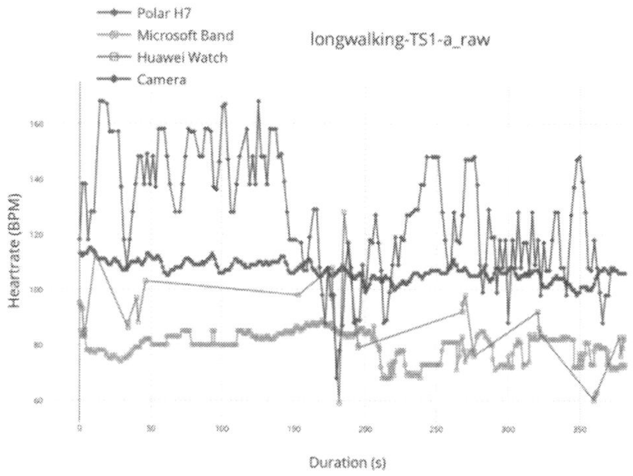

Figure 4. Heart rate measured during long walking.

are shown in these Figures. Because of practical reasons, it was not possible to measure heart rate with the Omrom M6 during physical activities in the fitness room.

For each device, we investigated trend and reactivity. Trend only judges a scoped-out-view of the heart rate signal based on the statistics average and correlation. Reactive is more strict and judges short periods of time. If an intense physical activity causes a sudden increase in heart rate, it is important that the sensor registers this increase. If a sensor is able to detect these sudden changes quickly, then it can be considered as highly reactive.

A. *Specialized device: sensor with chest strap*

The Polar H7 is considered as a reference. The output of the other devices is compared to the heart rate registered with the Polar.

B. *Fitness tracker*

The Microsoft Band 2 registers a heart rate that is consistently lower than the reference value of the Polar. This

TABLE I. HEART RATE MEASUREMENTS WITH TWO USERS (TS1 AND TS2) IN REST CONDITION AT TWO DIFFERENT TIMES

	TS1-1		TS1-2		TS2-1		TS2-2	
Device	$\bar{x} \pm \sigma$	median	$\bar{x} \pm \sigma$	median	$\bar{x} \pm \sigma$	median	$\bar{x} \pm \sigma$	median
Omrom M6	76±2.5	-	84±4.2	-	55±2.8	-	58±2.9	-
Polar H7	77±3.0	76	80±3.7	79	56±1.7	56	59±1.4	59
Huawei Watch	73±3.3	73	72±3.2	71	55±2.0	55	55±2.0	56
Microsoft Band	75±3.3	75	76±1.7	76	50±2.9	60	64±6.0	64

discrepancy varies for different heart rates, which makes it hard to correct. Moreover, measures of the Microsoft Band deviate substantially from the reference during intense activities. Figure 3 shows that the sensor has a low reactivity. Rapidly varying heart rates are not detected during the Dumbbell Curl exercise.

C. Smart watch

Because of interruptions in the measurement process due to movements, the number of measurement results obtained with the Huawei Watch is smaller than obtained with the Polar H7. Time periods without measurements correspond to periods of sensor (re)calibration due to movements of the wrist. As a result, this device shows to be less suitable for measuring heart rate during activities with a lot of movement (of the wrist).

In terms of accuracy, the results show a trend that corresponds to the reference of the Polar. The mean value is 5 beats per minute below the mean value of the Polar reference. But this difference is consistent for different heart rates which allows a correction by adding the fixed difference to the measurements. Figure 3 shows this smart watch has some difficulties in detecting physical activities with varying intensities. Intensive periods are noticeable in the measurement data; but a delay in the peaks of the data is visible if the Polar and Huawei are compared.

D. Secondary device feature: PPG on smartphone

Because of the physical movements, PPG on the smartphone is not possible during Dumbbell Curl exercises. Because of the algorithm's dependency on the hardware, fluctuations in the measurements can be witnessed, even for a stable heart rate. The trend of the PPG method matches with the measurements of the Polar device. The trend of PPG is even better than the trend of the smart watch and fitness tracker for an exercise with low variation in intensity, as shown in Figure 2. In other cases, the heart rate measurements obtained with PGG may significantly differ from the Polar reference, as visible in Figure 4.

VII. CONCLUSION AND FUTURE WORK

This paper investigated the accuracy of heart rate measurements with sensors in wearables and smartphones. Experiments showed that specialized devices, using a sensor with chest strap, produce very accurate results, similar to devices that are approved for medical purposes. Measurements with the fitness tracker and smart watch that were tested, showed very accurate results in conditions with little physical movement, e.g., in resting state. However, a discrepancy in measured heart rate is witnessed during periods with a highly variable heart rate, e.g., during high intensity interval training. This low reactivity is often due to physical movements of the wrist. Devices around the wrist may lose their reference during movement, and subsequently require a recalibration of the sensor for a few seconds. Measuring heart rate by using PPG on a smartphone showed fluctuating measurements, even in case of little physical movements. This might be due to changes in light intensity in the environment or movements of the finger. Aggregating multiple measurements showed that statistics, such as average and median, are a good representation of the real heart rate. Because of hardware dependent characteristics, algorithms using the PPG technique are often too general. The general applicability of the algorithms for PPG allows heart rate monitoring on different smartphone devices, but reduces the accuracy of the results. Although fitness trackers, smart watches, or PPG on smartphones are useful tools to get information about the heart rate, we experienced some inaccuracies in the measurements during physical movements or sudden variations in heart rate. For medical purposes or professional athletes, specialized devices with a chest strap might be a better choice because of their higher accuracy. In future work, we will investigate how to automatically detect physical exercises, such as squats, and couple these exercises to the heart rate for further analysis. For the detection of exercises, sensors of mobile devices, such as the accelerometer, will be used. Next, we plan to develop an eHealth recommender system offering personal suggestions for physical activities based on the measured heart rate and performed exercises.

ACKNOWLEDGMENT

The authors would like to thank Enias Cailliau for his extensive research and implementation work in the context of this study.

REFERENCES

[1] T. Bodenheimer, E. H. Wagner, and K. Grumbach, "Improving primary care for patients with chronic illness," Jama, vol. 288, no. 14, 2002, pp. 1775–1779.

[2] F. W. Booth, C. K. Roberts, and M. J. Laye, "Lack of exercise is a major cause of chronic diseases," 2011.

[3] S. Hammer, J. Kim, and E. André, "Med-styler: Metabo diabetes-lifestyle recommender," in Proceedings of the Fourth ACM Conference on Recommender Systems, ser. RecSys '10. New York, NY, USA: ACM, 2010, pp. 285–288.

[4] S. A. Khan et al., "Gethealthyharlem.org: developing a web platform for health promotion and wellness driven by and for the harlem community." AMIA. Annual Symposium proceedings / AMIA Symposium., vol. 2009, 2009, pp. 317–321.

[5] S. Chen, J. Lach, O. Amft, M. Altini, and J. Penders, "Unsupervised activity clustering to estimate energy expenditure with a single body sensor," in 2013 IEEE International Conference on Body Sensor Networks, May 2013, pp. 1–6.

[6] F. Dadashi et al., "A hidden markov model of the breaststroke swimming temporal phases using wearable inertial measurement units," in 2013 IEEE International Conference on Body Sensor Networks, May 2013, pp. 1–6.

[7] J. Low, "Consumer health informatics: Informing consumers and improving health care," D. Lewis, G. Eysenbach, R. Kukafka, P. Z. Stavri, and H. Jimison, Eds. Routledge, an imprint of Taylor & Francis Books Ltd, 2007, vol. 23, no. 5, pp. 415–416.

[8] R. J. Cline and K. M. Haynes, "Consumer health information seeking on the internet: the state of the art," Health education research, vol. 16, no. 6, 2001, pp. 671–692.

[9] G. Eysenbach, "Consumer health informatics," British medical journal, vol. 320, no. 7251, 2000, p. 1713.

[10] V. J. Strecher et al., "The effects of computer-tailored smoking cessation messages in family practice settings," Journal of Family Practice, vol. 39, no. 3, 1994, pp. 262–270.

[11] M. K. Campbell, B. M. DeVellis, V. J. Strecher, A. S. Ammerman, R. F. DeVellis, and R. S. Sandler, "Improving dietary behavior: the effectiveness of tailored messages in primary care settings," American journal of public health, vol. 84, no. 5, 1994, pp. 783–787.

[12] P. S. Freedson and K. Miller, "Objective monitoring of physical activity using motion sensors and heart rate," Research quarterly for exercise and sport, vol. 71, no. sup2, 2000, pp. 21–29.

[13] J. Kim, "Wearable heart rate monitors enter the consumer mainstream," 2014, retrieved: April, 2017, at http://internetofthingsagenda.techtarget.com/feature/Wearable-device-heart-rate-monitoring-entering-the-consumer-mainstream.

[14] L. Fernandez-Luque, R. Karlsen, and L. Vognild, "Challenges and opportunities of using recommender systems for personalized health education," Studies in health technology and informatics, vol. 150, 2008, pp. 903–907.

[15] K. Binsted, A. Cawsey, and R. Jones, Generating personalised patient information using the medical record. Berlin, Heidelberg: Springer Berlin Heidelberg, 1995, pp. 29–41.

[16] V. Strecher, M. Kreuter, D. Den Boer, S. Kobrin, H. Hospers, and C. Skinner, "The effects of computer-tailored smoking cessation messages in family practice settings," The Journal of family practice, vol. 39, no. 3, September 1994, pp. 262–270.

[17] D. Jannach, M. Zanker, A. Felfernig, and G. Friedrich, Recommender Systems: An Introduction, 1st ed. New York, NY, USA: Cambridge University Press, 2010.

[18] M. Beveridge and D. Milward, "Definition of the high-level task specification language. deliverable d11, eu 5th framework homey project," IST-2001-32434, Tech. Rep., 2003.

[19] T. Giorginoll, C. R. Quaglinil, and J. Baccheschi, "The homey project: a telemedicine service for hypertensive patients," Personalisation for e-Health, vol. 21, 2005, pp. 32–35.

[20] M. N. K. Boulos, A. C. Brewer, C. Karimkhani, D. B. Buller, and R. P. Dellavalle, "Mobile medical and health apps: state of the art, concerns, regulatory control and certification," Online journal of public health informatics, vol. 5, no. 3, 2014, p. 229.

[21] M. J. Handel, "mhealth (mobile health)using apps for health and wellness," EXPLORE: The Journal of Science and Healing, vol. 7, no. 4, 2011, pp. 256–261.

[22] L. van Velsen, D. J. Beaujean, and J. E. van Gemert-Pijnen, "Why mobile health app overload drives us crazy, and how to restore the sanity," BMC medical informatics and decision making, vol. 13, no. 1, 2013, p. 23.

[23] M. Weippert et al., "Comparison of three mobile devices for measuring r–r intervals and heart rate variability: Polar s810i, suunto t6 and an ambulatory ecg system," European journal of applied physiology, vol. 109, no. 4, 2010, pp. 779–786.

[24] R. R. Kroll, J. G. Boyd, and D. M. Maslove, "Accuracy of a wrist-worn wearable device for monitoring heart rates in hospital inpatients: A prospective observational study," Journal of medical Internet research, vol. 18, no. 9, 2016, p. 253.

[25] F. El-Amrawy and M. I. Nounou, "Are currently available wearable devices for activity tracking and heart rate monitoring accurate, precise, and medically beneficial?" Healthcare informatics research, vol. 21, no. 4, 2015, pp. 315–320.

[26] L. N. Katz and A. Pick, Clinical electrocardiography. Lea & Febiger, 1956.

[27] A. Anier, J. Kaik, and K. Meigas, "Device and methods for performing transesophageal stimulation at reduced pacing current threshold," Estonian Journal of Engineering, vol. 14, no. 2, 2008, pp. 154–166.

[28] A. Reisner, P. A. Shaltis, D. McCombie, and H. H. Asada, "Utility of the photoplethysmogram in circulatory monitoring," The Journal of the American Society of Anesthesiologists, vol. 108, no. 5, 2008, pp. 950–958.

[29] M. Altini, "Heart Rate Variability for Training," 2013, retrieved: April, 2017, at http://www.marcoaltini.com/blog/heart-rate-variability.

[30] Omron, "Automatic Blood Pressure Monitor - Model M6 Comfort IT," 2015, retrieved: April, 2017, at www.omron-healthcare.com/en/support/manuals/download/m6-comfort-it-hem-7322u-e-en.

[31] M. Altini, J. Penders, R. Vullers, O. Amft et al., "Automatic heart rate normalization for accurate energy expenditure estimation," Methods of information in medicine, vol. 53, no. 5, 2014, pp. 382–388.

[32] P. T. Katzmarzyk, "Physical activity, sedentary behavior, and health: paradigm paralysis or paradigm shift?" Diabetes, vol. 59, no. 11, 2010, pp. 2717–2725.

The Demographics of Social Media Users in the Russian-Language Internet

Sergey Vinogradov, Vera Danilova, Alexander Troussov and Sergey Maruev
International laboratory for mathematical modelling of social networks,
RANEPA,
Moscow, Russia
e-mails: derbosebar@gmail.com, maolve@gmail.com, troussov@gmail.com, Maruev@ranepa.ru

Abstract—**Our study focuses on the demography of the largest European social network VK and the representativeness of VK population sample with respect to the real-world state demography. The relationships between the variables, such as region code, settlement type, age and gender are explored. A special-purpose tool has been developed for ethnic group labeling purposes, which performs the classification given the user forename, patronymic and/or surname and ensures 99.2% accuracy. The analysis of the considered variables is helpful in finding a solution to the cold start problem in recommender systems.**

Keywords- internet sociology; internet demography; internet surveys; social network analysis.

I. INTRODUCTION

Scientists and politicians are concerned about the accuracy of traditional sociology's methods (questionnaires). Traditional polls are no longer a gold standard for the evaluation of politicians activity, elections outcome prediction and studies of voters' preferences. Predictions failed for the US 2016 elections, events in Israel, U.K. and Greece last year, Scottish independence referendum and US congress elections of 2014 [2]. As for the Internet surveys, the initial confidence in the accuracy of their methods was replaced by doubts about their consistency, mainly because (i) Internet demography differs from the real-world one, and (ii) demographies of different Internet segments vary significantly from one another, e.g., as of 2008, the Facebook audience was dominated by young white people from middle-class families, while MySpace was represented mainly by Afro-Americans [4]. Taking into account the discrepancies between the Internet demography and the real-world demography allows us to perform a more efficient study of potential customers, voters, patients and others on the Web and to apply the results to real-world situations.

Our study considers 239.044.903 user profiles of the largest European online social networking service VKontakte (VK) [28], whose average daily audience equals to 64.525.950. The study includes the following stages: (i) data collection via VK Open Application Programming Interface (API) [29]; (ii) filtering; (iii) user location identification using the Federal Information Address System (FIAS); (iv) analyzing the relationship between the variables: region code, settlement type, age and gender; (v) developing the ethnic group classifier for further use of the corresponding variable.

Current results include 1) the analysis of the age distribution of VK users across regions and settlement types, and 2) the analysis of the gender distribution of VK users across regions and settlement types. A tool for ethnic group labeling of target users has been developed and validated, so that the ethnic group feature can be further processed. An important application of our study of Social Network (SN) users demographics is to improve user profiling and mitigate the problem of the cold start in recommender systems (how to recommend a movie to see or a product to buy to new users with no history of activities).

The paper is organized as follows. Section II overviews the state of the art in the domain. Section III considers data gathering, filtering and description. In Section IV, the analysis of the obtained data is covered. Section V outlines the tool for ethnic group labeling and Section VI concludes the paper.

II. RELATED WORK

Among papers dealing with the study of Facebook and other English-speaking SN population are the works by 1) J. Chang et al. [5] on the study of ethnic groups represented in the SN, 2) P. Corbett [6] on Facebook demographic groups, 3) T. Strayhorn [23] on gender differences in the use of Facebook and Myspace by first-year college students.

Twitter data has been widely used for quantitative measurement and prediction of real-world events including prediction of the price level in the stock market [3], sentiment analysis of brands [21], prediction of movie revenues [1], earthquake prediction [20], and prediction of election outcomes [14] [27]. A large number of these predictions turned out to be inaccurate, which leads to the following questions: (i) Is Twitter population representative enough? (ii) In case it is, in which segments? Since Twitter-based predictions are considered to allow for a better understanding of real-world events and phenomena, Twitter sample should be representative to a certain extent: e.g., young people tweet far more often than older people, therefore, the corresponding part of the population is better represented. In any case, SN data analysis can be fruitful only if the SN demography data is approached scientifically.

One of the first papers on Twitter demography published by A. Mislove et al. [13] asked the following questions: (i) Who are Twitter users? (ii) To which extent the Twitter profile collection is representative of the whole population of the country? The authors undertook the first steps to explore the Twitter dataset that covers over 1% of the US population. A comparative study of the Twitter population and the real-world one was conducted based on 3 criteria: location, gender, race. It was shown that the SN population is non-uniformly distributed: densely populated regions are represented redundantly, while underpopulated regions representation is scarce. Moreover, the male population prevails on Twitter and results in a non-random sample.

Twitter has been selected as an example of social platform, because, as opposed to the users of other SNs, 91% of Twitter users made their profile and communication history visible to non-registered users. At the moment, Twitter data use is the only possibility to perform a free large-scale study of particular features of the communication and information exchange. The investigation of the Twitter platform started quite a long time ago and is being considered promising, however, there remain questions on the sufficiency of the representation of demographic groups in the sample. To compare Twitter data to the US Census 2000 data, users were mapped to their location (districts).

In [22], it was found out that most UK Twitter users prefer to indicate hobbies instead of their job. The authors explain it by the fact that the creative sector on Twitter is represented by an excessive number of users, as compared to the Census 2011 data. The tool for the automatic extraction of data on user age, developed by the authors, allowed to find out that, according to proportions, Twitter is dominated by young population as opposed to the Census 2011 data. However, in view of the predicted values, there is a significant number of older twitters. The study has shown that there is a way to extract the data on age and occupation of Twitter users from metadata with varying accuracy that depends particularly on professional groups.

III. Data

A. Collection

For the purposes of our study, 239 044 903 profiles from VK social network are considered. The data is accessed via VK Open API and collected using an in-house Python-based crawler. The gathered data is stored as JavaScript Object Notation (JSON) in a Hadoop cluster (HDFS) [11]. The processing is done using Apache Spark framework for in-memory cluster computing together with Hive data warehouse software [12].

B. Filtering

The following account types are excluded to sort out reliable data on the population of the considered social network: groups, deactivated accounts, fake accounts, and profiles, where no current city and/or no date of birth are indicated.

C. Description

As a result of data collection and filtering, two arrays are built. The first array in Comma-Separated Values (CSV) format contains 29.053 lines with the following information on VK population: location name, number of VK users, number of women among VK users, number of men among VK users, region code, location type (town, settlement or other). The second array in CSV format contains 1.048.576 lines with the following information on VK population: location name, age, number of VK users of this age, region code, location type.

The data was being collected during December 2015 for 83 regions, including the Moscow Region. The city of Moscow will be considered independently for comparison purposes in our future work. The information on user location is extracted from the "Current city" field in the general information section of user personal profiles. In the present work, we perform a comparison with the real demography (data from the official Federal State Statistics Service (Rosstat) statistics as of January 2015).

Each of the resulting nodes (non-fake profiles) is described by certain attributes, such as age, gender, settlement type, etc., that differ in format and dimensions. The majority of these attributes can be used for opinion mining, decision making in recommender systems, etc.. The main questions are: (i) how to evaluate the quality of these attributes? (ii) how to efficiently use them? To answer these questions, it is crucial to use the topology of the network where the given nodes live and communicate. We build a model, which, however imperfect, provides a high-resolution picture of the behavior of a large number of nodes (people). To evaluate the quality of attributes, the preferential connectivity coefficient is estimated: if nodes having a certain attribute connect more often, this attribute is considered useful. Attributes can be effectively used to study the structure of massive networks as it is shown in [24], where a method is introduced that automatically creates a network of overlapping clusters, from the largest to the smallest, up to a threshold of term frequencies that is used to detect the similarity of interests.

D. Filtering

The following account types are excluded to sort out reliable data on the population of the considered social network: groups, deactivated accounts, fake accounts, and profiles, where no current city and/or no date of birth are indicated.

IV. Data Analysis

The analysis is based on two types of the collected data: 1) gender distribution of users across regions and settlement types (49.334.562 users) and 2) age distribution of users across regions and settlement types (41.236.001 users). The information on the location of users is aligned with the FIAS data. The parameters of the above samples have the following differences. The first sample (gender distribution) includes the total number of users, the number of men, the number of women, the number of the region according to the Constitution and the settlement type corresponding to each of the settlements, where 83 regions and 35 settlement types are covered. The sample does not include the city of Moscow, Republic of Crimea and Sevastopol. The sample includes the city of Baikonur - one of the territories serviced by the Administration of secure facilities under the Ministry of Internal Affairs (No. 94 according to the Constitution and

No. 99 in our database). The second sample includes such parameters as age, the number of users of a given age, the number of the region according to the Constitution and the settlement type corresponding to each of the settlements, where 83 regions and 45 settlement types are covered. This sample does not include the city of Baikonur, the Republic of Crimea and Sevastopol.

The distribution of VK users among regions is presented in Figures 1 and 2. The plot is divided into two parts for visual clarity. The values are sorted from the smallest to the largest. The first plot is built in arithmetic scale (absolute values of the number of users), the second plot is built in logarithmic scale (the difference between the minimum and the maximum values in this area is over 8 millions). The fewest number of users (44) has been registered in the region defined by the number 99 in our database, which corresponds to Baikonur, a city leased from Kazakhstan until 2050. VK population under 10.000 has been registered in the following constituent regions: 33 - Vladimir Oblast (2148), 79 - Jewish Autonomous Oblast (2553), 6 - Republic of Ingushetia (6858).

The values change by 1-2 orders of magnitude in the range from 12.348 (87 - Chukotka Autonomous Okrug) to 262.389 (89 - Yamalo-Nenets Autonomous Okrug).

Figure 2 shows the demography of VK for the other 42 regions. The values change by one order of magnitude in the interval from 275.411 (40 - Kaluga Oblast) to 2.740.984 (66 - Sverdlovsk Oblast). The maximum value (8.377.856) is observed for Saint Petersburg (78).

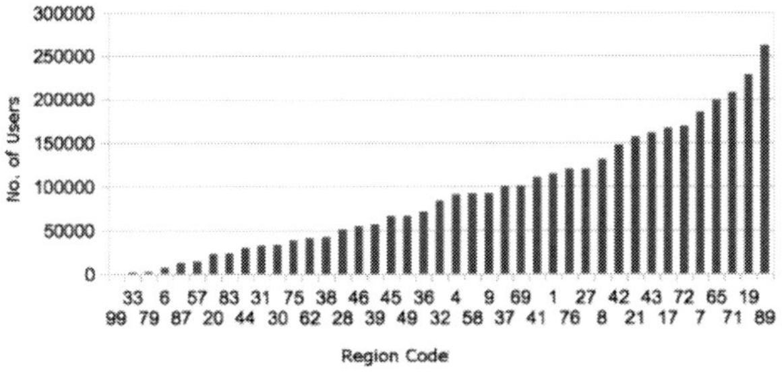

Figure 1. Distribution of the number of VK users among the constituent regions of the Russian Federation.

The real demography data has been taken from the Rosstat website [18]. The most recent statistics on the number of residents per region that can be accessed via the online Rosstat service reflects the situation as of January 1 of 2015, which allows us to perform the comparison with the data collected by our research group in December 2015. The results of the comparison of VK users distribution and the real Russian population distribution among the constituent regions are presented in Figures 3 and 4. These figures are parts of one plot. The first part describes data for the first 42 regions and the second part describes the remaining 40 regions, for a total of 82. The comparison is made for 82 regions, because Rosstat does not provide statistics for leased territories (Baikonur city). Moreover, the number of users in Baikonur is low (44). The comparison shows that, for most regions, the number of social network users is lower than the number of residents. For 30% of regions the number of registered users is the lowest (less than 10% of residents), as it is shown in Table I.

Furthermore, a relatively low number of VK users (under 20%) as compared to the number of residents is observed in the following constituent regions, as shown in Table II:

TABLE I. PERCENTAGE OF REGISTERED USERS PER REGION (1)

Region No.	Region Name	Percentage, %
33	Vladimir Oblast	0.15
6	Republic of Ingushetia	1.48
79	Jewish Autonomous Oblast	1.52
20	Chechen Republic	1.65
38	Irkutsk Oblast	1.74
57	Oryol Oblast	1.88
31	Belgorod Oblast	2.09
36	Voronezh Oblast	3.05
30	Astrakhan Oblast	3.23
75	Chita Oblast	3.54
62	Ryazan Oblast	3.59
44	Kostroma Oblast	4.56
72	Tyumen Oblast	4.72
46	Kursk Oblast	4.88
42	Kemerovo Oblast	5.40
39	Kaliningrad Oblast	5.86
28	Amur Oblast	6.31
32	Bryansk Oblast	6.77
58	Penza Oblast	6.79
45	Kurgan Oblast	7.59
69	Tver Oblast	7.65
27	Khabarovsk Krai	8.99
76	Yaroslavl Oblast	9.42
37	Ivanovo Oblast	9.67
24	Krasnoyarsk Krai	9.94

TABLE II. PERCENTAGE OF REGISTERED USERS PER REGION (2)

Region No.	Region Name	Percentage, %
43	Kirov Oblast	12.36
50	Moscow Oblast	12.56
21	Chuvash Republic	12.66
71	Tula Oblast	13.72
16	Tatarstan Republic	15.75
2	Bashkortostan Republic	16.28
5	Republic of Dagestan	17.05
9	Karachay-Cherkess Republic	19.64

The number of users in Moscow Oblast is quite low, according to the gathered data, probably because Moscow Oblast residents work and spend most of their time in the city of Moscow, so they prefer to specify "Moscow" as their current city. The situation will become clearer when we analyze the VK population in the city of Moscow.

In the following regions, the majority of residents have VK profiles: 3 - Republic of Buryatia (89.82%), 10 - Republic of Karelia (83.78%), 18 - Udmurt Republic (86.64%), 48 - Lipetsk Oblast (77.02%), 54 - Novosibirsk Oblast (75.83%).

The above considered regions, where we observe the excess of real demography statistics values, are situated in the Northwestern Federal District. Vologda Oblast is a highly industrialized region, where one of the largest metallurgical plants of the country (Severstal) is located. The metallurgical industry is followed by chemical, food (center of butter industry), timber and machine building industries. Also, salt production, glass making and textile industries are well developed.

Figure 2 shows the demography of VK for the other 42 regions. The values change by one order of magnitude in the interval from 275.411 (40 - Kaluga Oblast) to 2.740.984 (66 - Sverdlovsk Oblast). The maximum value (8.377.856) is observed for Saint Petersburg (78).

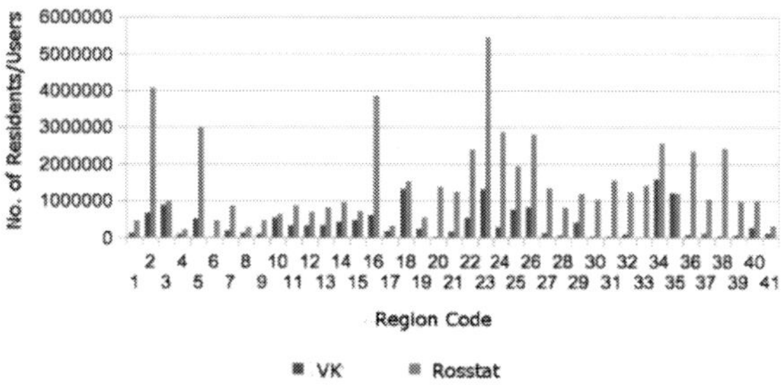

Figure 2. Comparison of the distribution of VK population through regions to the official Rosstat statistics as of January 1st, 2015 (1).

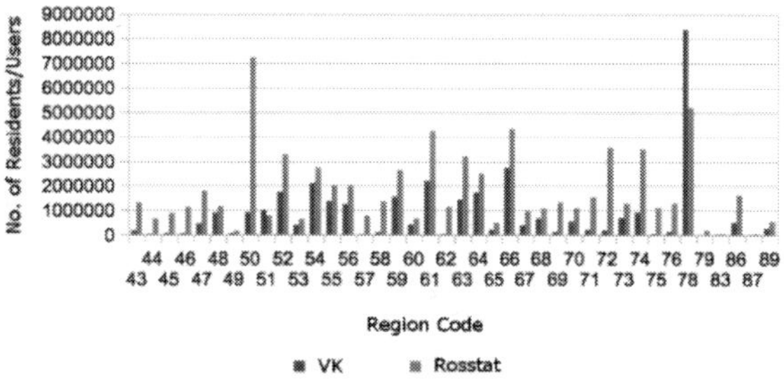

Figure 3. Comparison of the distribution of VK population through regions to the official Rosstat statistics as of January 1st, 2015 (2).

Murmansk Oblast is the home of one of the largest Russian ports; therefore, the fishing industry is well developed here. These regions afford good job opportunities, they are always in need of qualified human resources. Having these circumstances in mind, the excess in the number of users compared to that of real residents can be partially explained by the possible recent movement of people corresponding to the indicated percentage of VK users to their new workplaces, which is why they have not yet been officially registered. As for Saint Petersburg, these users can be among those, who reside in this constituent region without a temporary residence permit nor an official workplace. Moreover, residents of Leningrad Oblast may have indicated "Saint Petersburg" in their current city field, because most of them work and spend most of their time there. Also, users may have selected Saint Peterburg, because they plan to move there in the nearest future and/or they do it on purpose to attract attention from other users. The distribution of VK users according to the settlement (locality) type is presented in Figures 5, 6, 7 and 8. Figure 5 shows the extent to which urban population prevails over that of other settlement types (46.803.588 citizens against 2.530.974 (5.13%) in rural settlements, Cossack villages, mountain villages and other).

In Figure 6, the VK population in a range of settlements is presented, where cities and settlement types with population under one thousand users are excluded for visual clarity. The standard notation for settlement types is transliterated (sl - sloboda, kp - health resort settlement, gorodok - community area, st and zd/d st - train station, aul - mountain village, u - ulus (administrative division of the Sakha Republic), np - inhabited locality (settlement), kh - khutor (a type of rural locality in Eastern Europe), st-tsa - Cossack village, rp - workers' settlement, p - settlement, pgt - small town, d - small village, s - big village).

Figure 4. VK users distribution according to settlement type.

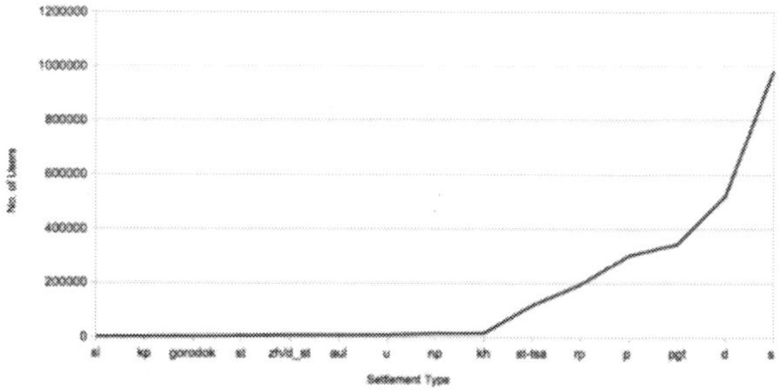

Figure 5. VK social network population distribution across different settlement types.

Population values for settlement types between sloboda and khutor change smoothly from 1427 to 15113. In the khutor - big village, the interval population values change drastically from 15113 to 985069.

Figures 7 and 8 show VK population values for all of the considered settlement types in logarithmic scale, organized from the smallest to the largest. The standard notation of settlement types is used (the list of settlement types can be found in [19]. The notation is as follows: s/a - rural administration, zh/d op - railway station, sh - highway, zh/d post - railway post, zh/d rzd - railway junction, s/o - rural okrug, r-n - district, dp - suburban settlement, s/s - rural council, p/o - post office, p/st - settlement near a railway station. The lowest population has been registered for the following settlement types: s/a - 1 user, zh/d op - 3 users, zh/d post - 4 users, sh - 4 users. In the s/a - p/o interval the population grows by 3 orders of magnitude to 628 users (p/o).

Furthermore, in the p/st - bv range it changes by 3 orders of magnitude from 675 to 985069 users. So, the leading settlement types as to the number of VK users are (in descending order) city, big village, small village, small town, settlement, workers' settlement, Cossack village.

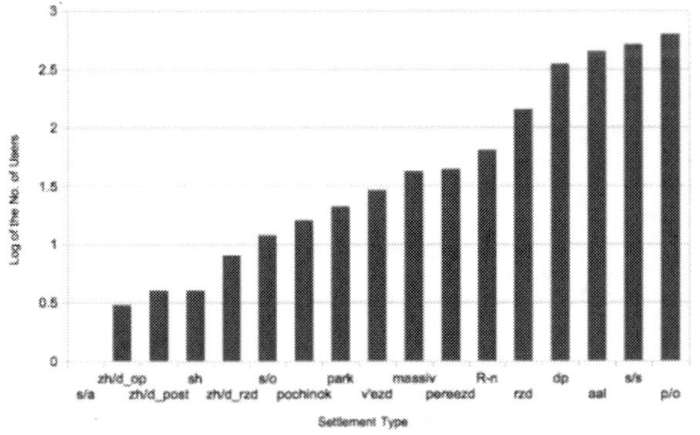

Figure 6. Quantitative distribution of VK social network users according to the settlement type (1).

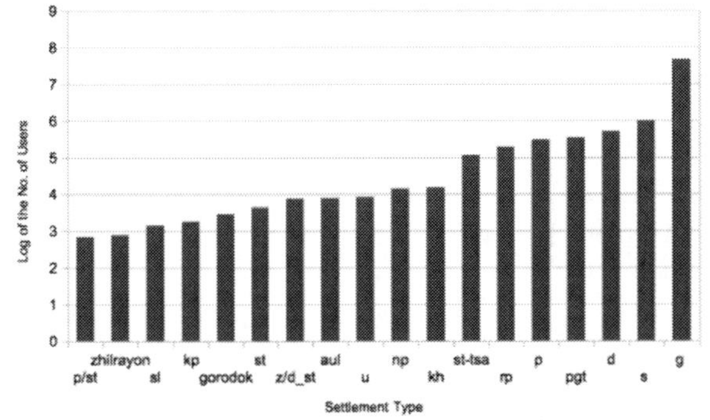

Figure 7. Quantitative distribution of VK social network users according to the settlement type (2).

A. *Gender*

Gender distribution of VK users across regions is depicted in Figures 9 and 10 (percentage ratio). The number of men is marked with blue color, the number of women - with orange color. According to the obtained data, in 19 out of 82 regions most users indicated gender in their profiles (Table III).

TABLE III. PERCENTAGE OF THE USERS THAT INDICATED GENDER IN THEIR PROFILE

Region No.	Region Name	Percentage, %
3	Republic of Buryatia	75.34
48	Lipetsk Oblast	76.05
64	Saratov Oblast	76.13
56	Orenburg Oblast	76.28
18	Udmurt Oblast	76.89
68	Tambov Oblast	77.54
51	Murmansk Oblast	77.83
15	North Osetia Republic	78.14
74	Chelyabinsk Oblast	78.31
63	Samara Oblast	79.35
24	Krasnoyarsk Oblast	85.45
35	Vologda Oblast	85.91
22	Altai Krai	86.05
42	Kemerovo Oblast	86.95
47	Leningrad Oblast	89.60
23	Krasnodar Krai	93.94
61	Rostov Oblast	95.78
50	Moscow Oblast	97.98
52	Nizhniy Novgorod Oblast	98.70

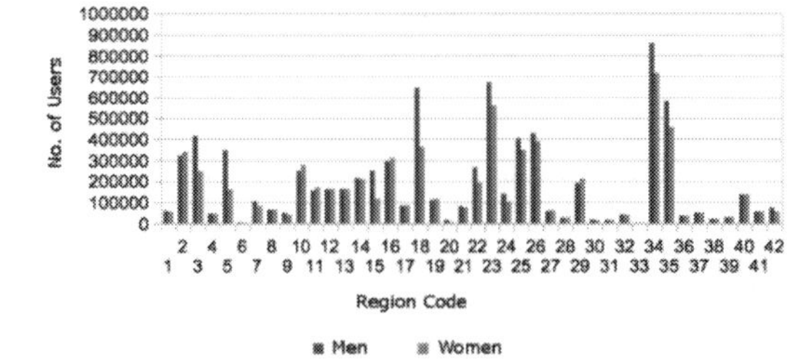

Figure 8. Gender distribution of VK social network users across regions (1).

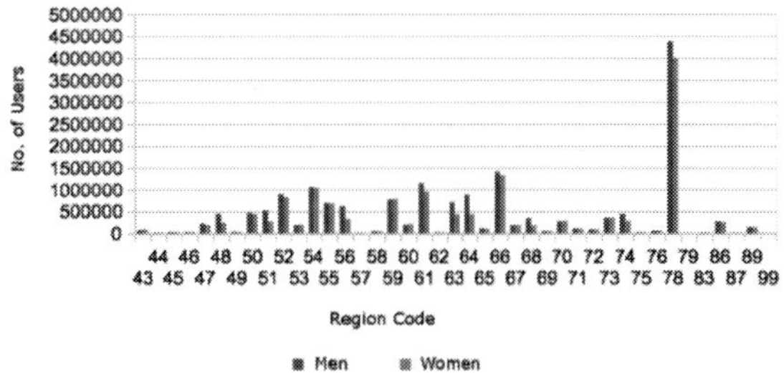

Figure 9. Gender distribution of VK social network users across regions (2).

In 40 of the considered regions, over 50% of users are men. Region 99 (Baikonur city) cannot be taken into account in the gender analysis, because only 44 users are registered there as of December 2015 and 30 of them are men. The lowest number of male users has been observed in Yamalo-Nenets Autonomous Okrug 83 (46.34%). Also, this value is lower in the following constituent regions: 6 - Republic of Ingushetia (68.14%), 5 - Republic of Dagestan (68.35%), 20 - Chechen Republic (74.03%). In 58 regions there are less than 50% of female users. The highest number of female users (53.65%) resides in Yamalo-Nenets Autonomous Okrug (83). In the following constituent regions women constitute less than 30% of users: 15 - North Osetia Republic (24.62%), 64 - Saratov Oblast (24.80%), 20 - Chechen Republic (25.29%), 51 - Murmansk Oblast (25.98%), 48 - Lipetsk Oblast (26.23%), 68 - Tambov Oblast (26.43%), 56 - Orenburg Oblast (26.46%), 18 - Udmurt Oblast (27.64%), 3 - Republic of Buryatia (28.12%), 74 - Chelyabinsk Oblast (29.79%), 63 - Samara Oblast (29.88%). According to the processed data on VK demography, the number of men in this social network is 3.970.836 higher than the number of women.

B. Age

The following account types are excluded to sort out reliable data on the population of the considered social network: groups, deactivated accounts, fake accounts, and profiles, where no current city and/or no date of birth are indicated.

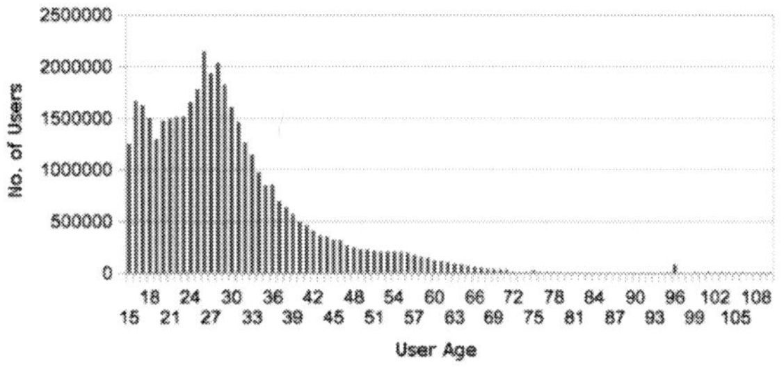

Figure 10. Age distribution of VK users across regions.

Age distribution of VK social network users across regions is shown in Figure 11. Most users are from 15 to 33 years old. The peaks are achieved at age 26 (2.145.219) and 28 (2.031.442). In what follows, the higher the age value, the lower the number of users. However, there is an unusual maximum at the age of 96. Most probably, users chose this age at random.

A comparison with Rosstat data has been conducted (see Figures 12 and 13).

It is important to note that the VK sample includes only those users whose profiles contain age data. The sum of all users that show (or fake) their age constitutes 41.236.001, while the sum of all Russian Federation residents with the age attribute recorded in Rosstat database is 121.861.482. The comparison shows that the main maximums stay close for both samples: the majority of users/residents are of ages 26-28. According to Rosstat calculations, the number of residents of age 27 is the highest (2.607.083). Also, there are over 2 million residents with the age values 23-42, 44 and 51-60 in Russian Federation. Only two age values exceed 2 million users (26 and 28 years old) and the age corresponding to the most VK users is 26 (2.145.219 users).

TABLE IV. EXCESS IN THE NUMBER OF VK USERS COMPARED TO THE OFFICIAL NUMBER OF RESIDENTS, ACCORDING TO ROSSTAT

Age	Excess, No. of People	Percentage, %
16	311.207	23%
17	307.609	23.4%
18	113.946	8.2%
96	67.320	406.87%
99	4.479	83.42%

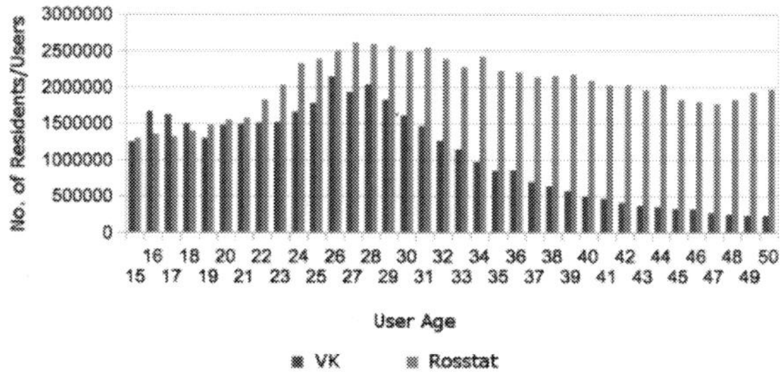

Figure 11. Comparison of VK and Rosstat data on age distribution (1).

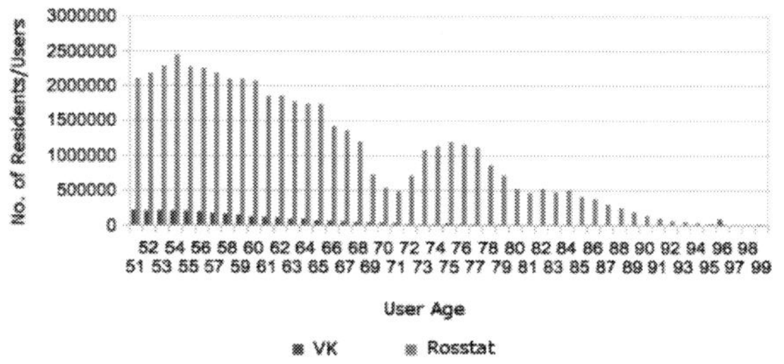

Figure 12. Comparison of VK and Rosstat data on age distribution (2).

Age distribution of rural and urban population, as well as the comparison of VK and official Rosstat statistics is presented in Figures 14, 15, 16 and 17.

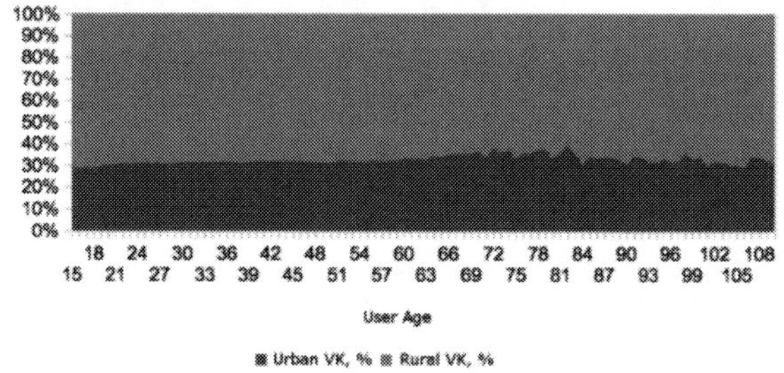

Figure 13. Age percentage distribution of urban and rural VK population.

According to the processed data for the second sample, the amount of urban VK population is significantly lower than that of rural population (Figure 14). In general, urban population equals to 30.81% and rural population - to 69.19% of the total population (41.236.001 users). Values are in the range from 28.67% (17 years) to 39.21% (82 years), the average value is 32.51%. It turns out that the least number of users of age 17 live in towns/cities and over 40% of users at the age of 82 are urban citizens as well. Surprisingly, the same ratio is observed for all of the considered ages (15-110). Since we have been expecting the opposite results, there will be another iteration of data collection process to build a new age distribution across different settlement types. A detailed examination of the sample gives us an idea on the origins of these results. Only 316 out of 1114 towns and cities of the Russian Federation (data as of January 1st, 2015[31]) form part of our sample. The complete list of towns and cities has been taken from [16]. When comparing the lists, we have found out that our automatically created list of town/city names includes wrong entries that probably refer to some areas/objects (district, street, metro station, etc.) inside a town/city or suburban area, such as "Roshcha", "Malaya", "Yuzhnaya", "Yuzhny", "Chekhov-1", "Chekhov-4", "Chekhov-5", "Chekhov-6", "Chekhov-7", "Druzhba", "Kirova", "Krutaya", "Krutoy", "Lenina", "Nizhniy", "Nizhnyaya", which do not correspond to any of the entries in the official list.

Figure 15 shows the age distribution of rural and urban population of the Russian Federation, according to the official Rosstat information, based on the data on 121.861.482 residents, which is 3 times higher than the considered number of VK users. The urban population of the Russian Federation is 2.95 higher than that of rural population as of January 1st, 2015. Rural population constitutes only 25.30% of the total population.

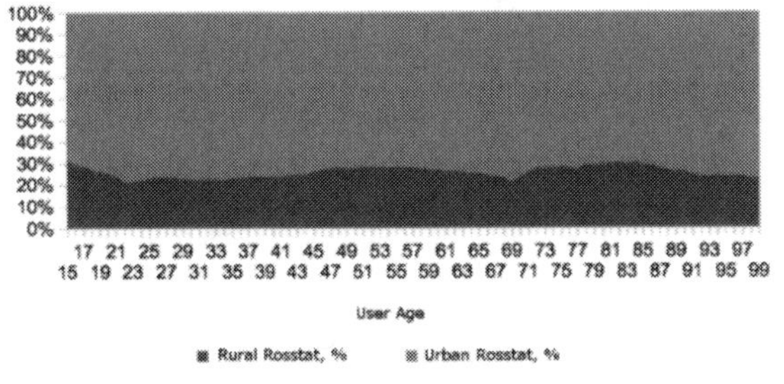

Figure 14. Age percentage distribution of urban and rural population, according to Rosstat.

Figure 16 shows age distribution of the Russian Federation rural population, according to VK API data as compared to Rosstat calculations. The number of users between 15 and 37 years residing in the rural area is higher than that of the registered rural residents in this age interval (almost 2 times higher in the 15-31 range). In what follows, as the age value increases, the number of users smoothly decreases in the range from 37 to 99 years, except the previously seen unusual peak at 96 years: the number of rural residents at the age of 96 (57.424) is significantly higher than that of the officially registered Russian Federation residents at this age (3.952).

Figure 17 depicts the comparative age distribution of the Russian Federation urban population, according to VK API data as compared to Rosstat calculations. As it has been noticed before, VK urban population sample is not representative enough, which is why another iteration of data collection and analysis is needed. On the basis of the processed data, we conclude that urban population of ages between 15 and 34 prevails (from 300.000). School and university students turn out to be the most active part of VK users: 909.412 users at the age between 15 and 25 years (in total) against 666.719 at the age between 26 and 99 years (in total). In the following, as the age grows, the VK urban population smoothly decreases (34-99 years), except the maximum at the age of 96, where the obtained value (26.424) is higher than the official statistics (12.594) as in the case of rural population.

While comparing VK and Rosstat plots, we have noticed that the largest number of users/residents is observed in the interval between 25 and 30 years in both cases: over 500.000 VK users between 24 and 30 years and around 2.000.000 officially registered residents between 27 and 29.

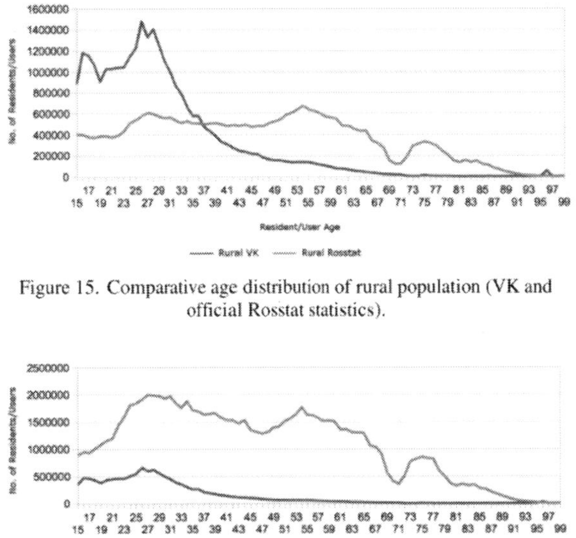

Figure 15. Comparative age distribution of rural population (VK and official Rosstat statistics).

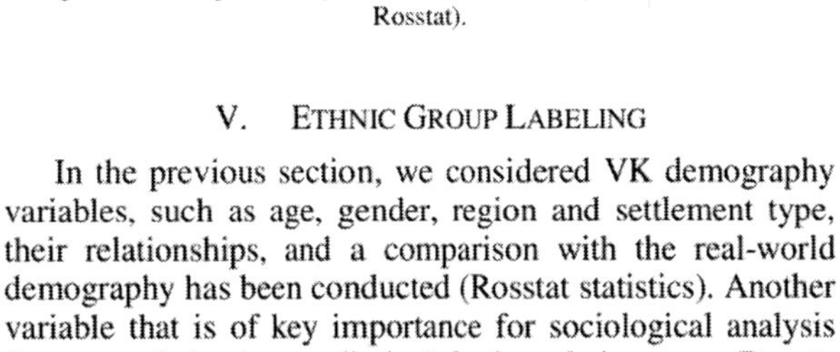

Figure 16. Comparative age distribution of urban population (VK and Rosstat).

V. Ethnic Group Labeling

In the previous section, we considered VK demography variables, such as age, gender, region and settlement type, their relationships, and a comparison with the real-world demography has been conducted (Rosstat statistics). Another variable that is of key importance for sociological analysis (e.g., user behavior prediction) is the ethnic group. Due to the fact that this parameter is not indicated in SN profiles, our task is to devise an algorithm for the automatic classification of users according to their ethnic group. We plan to compare the results with the official data on the ethnic composition of the Russian Federation [30].

Our tool for ethnic group labeling takes forename, patronymic, if any, and surname data as input and outputs the ethnic affiliation. It has been successfully tested on the lists of eminent people (e.g., Time's magazine list of 100 most important people of the 20th Century [26], famous Georgians [7], Ossetians [17], List of People's Artists of Azerbaijan [32], etc.). The average accuracy of the system is 99.2%. The core of the algorithm is a neural network trained on representative samples. The existing similar-purpose systems of the prior art are Onolytics [15], E-tech [8], EthnicSeer [10], Ethnea [9] and TextMap [25].

These systems use predefined hierarchies/group lists, however, no hierarchy/list construction standards are mentioned. Except for Wikipedia, no training resources are referenced in case of machine learning-based systems. Moreover, the hierarchies represent a mix of ethnic and religious (e.g., "Muslim" is listed as an ethnic group) groups. Russian ethnic diversity is not covered by these hierarchies/lists, therefore, a special-purpose structure has been developed. The details on the classification algorithm and comparison to the similar-purpose systems will be given in an upcoming paper.

VI. Conclusions And Future Work

This paper presents the first steps toward understanding the attributes of social media users. It includes the analysis of VK social network population sample and the comparison to Rosstat data. The attributes taken into account include region code, settlement type, age and gender. VK covers the following regions the best (in descending order): Saint Petersburg, Murmansk Oblast, Vologda Oblast, Republic of Buryatia, Republic of Karelia, Udmurt Republic, Lipetsk Oblast, Novosibirsk Oblast. According to the first sample that takes into account the gender feature, the urban VK population is 18 times larger than the rural one. The number of men in VK is 3.970.836 higher than the number of women. The majority of VK users indicated their gender in 19 out of 82 regions, including Murmansk Oblast (77.83%), Vologda Oblast (85.91%), Republic of Buryatia (75.34%), Udmurt Oblast (76.89%) and Lipetsk Oblast (76.05%) that are among the best covered by VK. According to the second sample including users that specified their age, most VK users are between 15 and 33 years old. The number of users who specified their age in VK is 3 times lower than the official number of Russian Federation residents. The number of users of age 16-18, 96 and 99 exceeds the official number of residents with these age values. 81.159 VK users introduced the age in the interval from 100 to 110 years. For these age values there are no official statistics. Also, in the age-oriented VK sample, the rural population is two times higher than the urban one.

The ethnic group feature will also be considered upon additional testing of the corresponding tool. Our current tasks include comparing the ethnic composition of VK with the official data on the Russian Federation ethnic composition and assessing the name feature quality (whether it is useful for the analysis of user groups behavior and preferences, and, consequently, whether profiles can be improved using kins and/or friends profiles data). Also, we are developing an approach to effectively assess the quality of other account attributes. It can be helpful in mitigating the cold start problem in recommender systems.

References

[1] S. Asur and B. Huberman, "Predicing the future with social media," 2010, URL: http://arxiv.org/abs/1003.5699 [retrieved: September, 2016].

[2] "Bloomberg: European Edition," URL: http://www.bloombergview.com/quicktake/perils-of-polling [retrieved: December, 2016].

[3] J. Bollen, H. Mao, and X.-J. Zeng, "Twitter mood predicts the stock market," in Proceedings of ICWSM, 2010, pp. 1-8.

[4] D. Boyd, "Taken out of context: American teen sociality in networked publics," PhD thesis, University of California, Berkeley, 2008, URL: http://oskicat.berkeley.edu/record=b18339028~S1 [retrieved: November, 2015].

[5] J. Chang, I. Rosenn, L. Backstrom, and C. Marlow, "ePluribus: Ethnicity on Social Networks," Artificial Intelligence, 2010, pp. 18-25.

[6] P. Corbett, "Facebook demographics and statistics report 2010," 2010, URL: http://www.istrategylabs.com/2010/01/ facebook-demographics-and-statistics-report-010-145-growth- in-1-year [retrieved: June, 2016].

[7] "Famous Georgians," http://www.countries.ru/?pid=1950 [retrieved: November, 2016].

[8] "E-tech," URL:http://www.ethnictechnologies.com [retrieved: September, 2016].

[9] "Ethnea," URL:http://abel.lis.illinois.edu/cgi-bin/ethnea/search.py?Fname=kim&Lname=jung [retrieved: September, 2016].

[10] "EthnicSeer," URL:http://singularity.ist.psu.edu/ethnicity?name=kim+ jung&commit=Analyze [retrieved: September, 2016].

[11] "HDFS Architecture Guide," URL: https://hadoop.apache.org/docs/r1.2. 1/hdfs design.html) [retrieved: June, 2016].

[12] "Hive on Spark: Getting Started - Apache Hive - Apache Software Foundation", URL:https://cwiki.apache.org/confluence/display/Hive/Hive+ on+Spark%3A+Getting+Started [retrieved: June, 2016].

[13] A. Mislove, S. L. Jorgensen, Y-Y. Ahn, J-P. Onnela, and J. N. Rosenquist, "Understanding the demographics of Twitter users," in Proceedings of the Fifth International AAAI Conference on Weblogs and Social Media, AAAI Press, 2011, pp. 554-557.

[14] B. O'Connor, R. Balasubramanyan, B. Routledge, and N. Smith, "From tweets to polls: Linking text sentiment to public opinion time series," in Proceedings of the Fourth International AAAI Conference on Weblogs and Social Media, 2010, pp. 122-129.

[15] "Onolytics," URL:http://onolytics.com [retrieved: September, 2016]

[16] "Official Russian Cities List," URL: http://hramy.ru/regions/city abc. htm [retrieved: December, 2016].

[17] "Ossetians," URL: http://ossetians.com [retrieved: December, 2016].

[18] "Rosstat Federal State Statistics Service: Demography", URL: http://www.gks.ru/wps/wcm/connect/rosstat

main/rosstat/ru/statistics/ population/demography/ [retrieved: June, 2016].

[19] "Rosreestr. The Federal Service for State Registration, Cadastre and Cartography," URL: https://rosreestr.ru/upload/documenty/doc Pril 1 k P48.PDF [retrieved: June, 2016].

[20] T. Sakaki, M. Okazaki, and Y. Matsuo, "Earthquake shakes Twitter users: realtime event detection by social sensors," presented at WWW 2010, Raleigh, NC USA, 2010, pp. 851-860.

[21] M. Scarfi, "Social Media and the Big Data Explosion," in Forbes, 2012, URL:http://forbes.com/sites/onmarketing/2012/06/28/social-media-and-the-big-data-explosion/ [retrieved: September, 2016].

[22] L. Sloan, J. Morgan, P. Burnap, and M. Williams, "Who Tweets? Deriving the Demographic Characteristics of Age, Occupation and Social Class from Twitter User Meta-Data," PLoS ONE 10(3): e0115545, 2015, pp. 1-20, doi:10.1371/journal.pone.0115545.

[23] T. Strayhorn, "Sex differences in use of facebook and myspace among first-year college students," Stud. Affairs 10(2), 2009, URL: https: //www.studentaffairs.com/Customer-Content/www/CMS/files/Journal/Sex-Differences-in-Use-of-Facebook-and-MySpace.pdf[retrieved: June, 2016].

[24] A. Troussov, S. Maruev, S. Vinogradov, and M. Zhizhin, "Spreading Activation Connectivity Based Approach to Network Clustering," in Graph Theoretic Approaches for Analyzing Large-Scale Social Networks, N. Meghanathan (ed) IGI Global, 2017 (in print).

[25] "TextMap," URL:http://www.textmap.com/ethnicity/ September, 2016].

[26] "Time Magazine: 100 Most Important the 20th Century," URL: http://www.ranker.com/list/time-magazine-100-most-important-people-of-the-20th-century/theomanlenz [retrieved: December, 2016].

[27] A. Tumasjan, T. O. Sprenger, P. G. Sandner, and I. M. Welpe, "Predicting elections with Twitter: what 140 characters reveal about political sentiment," in Proceedings of the Fourth International AAAI Conference on Weblogs and Social Media, 2010, pp. 178-185.

[28] "VK," URL: http://vk.com [retrieved: June, 2016].

[29] "VK Open API," URL: https://vk.com/dev/openapi [retrieved: June, 2016].

[30] "Wikipedia: Ethnic groups in Russia", URL: https://ru.wikipedia.org/ wiki/Ethnic groups in Russia [retrieved: June, 2016].

[31] "Wikipedia: List of cities and towns in Russia," URL:https://ru. wikipedia.org/wiki/List of cities and towns in Russia [retrieved: June, 2016].

[32] "Wikipedia: List of People's Artists of Azerbaijan," URL: https: //en.wikipedia.org/wiki/List of People%27s Artists of Azerbaijan [retrieved: December, 2016].

Identifying Cyclic Words with the Help of Google Books N-grams Corpus

Costin – Gabriel Chiru, Vladimir – Nicolae Dinu
Department of Computer Science and Engineering
Politehnica University from Bucharest
Bucharest, Romania
E-mail: costin.chiru@cs.pub.ro, vladimir.dinu92@yahoo.com

Abstract—**In this paper, we present an application for identifying English words whose use is cyclic or regularly varies in time. The purpose of the developed application was to build a cross-platform system for indexing and analyzing the graphs of words usage over time. For words indexing, we used the data provided by the Google Books N-grams Corpus, which was afterwards filtered using the WordNet lexical database. For identifying the cyclic or regularly varying words, we used two different algorithms: autocorrelation and dynamic time warping. The results of the analysis can be visualized using a web interface. The application also offers the possibility to view the evolution of the use frequency of different words in time.**

Keywords-cyclicity detection; dynamic time warping; autocorrelation; Google Books N-grams Corpus; WordNet.

I. INTRODUCTION

This paper presents an application capable of indexing and analyzing the unigrams dataset from Google Books N-grams Corpus [1] for establishing which are the words that vary regularly in time, following a cyclic pattern. The analysis is done based on the graphs generated from the number of uses of each word in the publications from 1800 until 2008 that were indexed by Google. The results provided by the application are the words that were identified as being cyclic, along with the years where these words were cyclic and with the length of the cycle in years after which the pattern repreats.

The identification of cyclic words may prove useful in predicting many types of events, starting from the meaning of the cyclic word that was found. For example, if the word is a generic type of events, such as "rebellion", "revolution" or "war", they might suggest that such an event is about to happen. These results could also be used in the economic field, since if the word represents a salable product, it is possible that the public interest in that product has grown, and thus both sales and stocks of companies selling that product will possibly grow.

The paper continues with a short presentation of the researches developed starting from the Google Books Ngram Corpus. In Section 3, we present the details of our application, along with the data sources used, and afterwards we detail the two algorithms used for the identification of the cyclic words. Section 5 contains the obtained results and a comparison of the used algorithms from the perspective of these results. The paper ends with our final conclusions and with our plan to continue this research.

II. SIMILAR APPROACHES

In [2], the authors analyzed the evolution of 107 words from English, Spanish and Hebrew over 208 years (from 1800 to 2008). The purpose of this research was to highlight the co-evolution of language and culture. The pronounced changes seen in the language dynamic during the conflict periods revealed the fact that the correlations that appear between words in time are influenced by co-evolutionary social, technological and political factors. The authors conclude that the birth of different words is most commonly related to new social and technological trends. Moreover, a new word requires some time to get into regular use and the authors established this period to be of 30-50 years.

Roth [3] examined the role of different autonomous function systems (such as the economy, science, art, religion, etc.) in 3 different societies (English, French and German) with the purpose of ranking these systems according to the public oppinion. He assumed that the public oppinion related to each such system may be expressed as the number of times words related to that system were used each year. In this sense, he used the graphs offered by Google Ngram Books Viewer to visualize the evolution in the use frequencies for the words related to the functional systems during 1800 and 2000. The results showed that even though everybody speaks about the economization, fact supported by the increase use of terms from the economic domain, the ascending tendencies of these terms stopped in each of the analyzed languages before reaching a dominant position. Moreover, for English, at the beginning, law was the dominant functional system, followed by religion and arts, while in the end policy was the main system, followed by law, health and education. For French, initially art ranked first, followed by religion, justice and policy. At the end of the analysis, on an ascending trend can be found policy, followed by art and economy. In the German case, the early 19th century was dominated by law as well as science, art, and religion. At the end of the analyzed period, policy was the main functional system, followed by legal system, art and science.

Acerbi et al. [4] analyzed the trend in using emotional words in the 20th century books using six lists of terms denoting fellings (such as anger, disgust, fear, happiness, sadness and surprise) that were previously used in a study on Twitter. The initial study revealed that changes in the frequency of use of different emotional words are caused by major events from human life, such as the death of a popular person, public tensions or natural disasters. Therefore, the authors hoped that, by using Google Books Ngram Corpus, they will be able to extend the proportion of the study.

The results of the study showed a descending trend in using emotional words in the last century, except for the last half, when, in american books can be seen an increase in the use of emotional words, compared to british books. Corroborated with this, the authors also investigated the difference between words and phrases related to the individual (e.g., independent, individual, unique, self, solitary, personal) and to the collective (e.g., team, collectively, set, group, union) showing that the former category has seen a great increase in american books during 1960 and 2008, while the others did not.

Another conclusion of the study is that there can be distinguished periods of happiness and sadness and that these periods are correlated with important historical events: the sadness peak corresponds to the WWII, while for happiness there are two peaks, one in 1920 and the other in 1960. Morerecently, it can be observed a sadness period starting in 1970 with an increase in hapiness in the last years of study.

Google Books Ngram Corpus was used in [5] to help compare different methods for estimating word relatedness. The authors used this corpus as common corpus for six corpus-based methods (Jaccard coefficient, Simpson Coefficient, Dice Coefficient, Pointwise Mutual Information, Normalized Google Distance and Relatedness based on Tri-grams). Afterwards, they compared the results obtained by the six methods on this corpus with the human ratings provided for some synonymy pairs. The comparison showed that the most accurate method is the Relatedness based on Tri-grams, which led to a Pearson correlation coefficient of 0.916. In the same time, the research proved the accuracy of the data from the Google Corpus, and stated the fact that all the analyzed metrics could be used on the n-grams offered by Google.

Another study, conducted by Wijaya and Yeniterzi [6] had the purpose to analyze the changes that occured in the meaning of a word over time. For that, they decided to analyze the evolution of the meaning of the words co-occurring with it over time. Thus, they used k-means clustering along with topic modelling over time, a topic modelling that has the advantage of using time as an explicit factor influencing the structure of a document.

As it can be seen from the above researches, time series analysis built on the data provided by Google Corpus has been used for various purposes, but none of them is similar to the approach proposed in this paper.

III. Implementation Details

A. Used Resources

For this research, we used data from two important sources: Google Books N-grams Corpus and WordNet.

1) Google Books N-grams Corpus

The data used in this project was extracted from the Google Books N-grams Corpus [1]. The corpus, created in 2009, contains the words written in over 5 million books published between 1500 and 2008. The corpus is made of over 500 billion words in 7 languages: English, French, German, Spanish, Hebrew, Russian and Chinese.

In this research, we only used the unigrams dataset from the corpus, this being formed with two types of files: the ones containing on each line information about the number of uses of a different word, and another one containing the total of words indexed for each year, that is used for normalization.

Although many researchers turned to this corpus for their experiments, there are also scientist criticizing it due to the errors generated by Optical Character Recognition (OCR) algorithms used to digitize content that was not digitally available. Another critique of this corpus is related to the insufficient data that it contains, only about 4% of all the books ever published being included in the corpus, thus lacking to offer a good coverage of all topics.

The corpus authors acknowledge these shortcomings and mention that the dataset is more relevant starting with 1800. Thus, we will restrict our analysis to the period 1800 -2008.

2) WordNet

The second data source for this research is represented by the WordNet lexical base [7] built at Princeton University. It contains only English words grouped based on their part-of-speech (nouns, verbs, adjectives and adverbs) and on their semantic, clustering words with similar meaning in synsets.

B. Modularization

The architecture of this application follows a three-tiers organization, with the data access module on the first tier, the services modules for offering the functionalities on the second (the logic tier) and the presentation tier, viewed by the user, which contains three modules: the indexer, the analyzer and the graphical user interface (the GUI of the application).

1) Data Access Module

This module contains the access logic to the tables from the database. The database contains a table "total", which saves the data referring to the entire unigram corpus used in this research; 26 tables (one for each letter) containing the words starting with that letter; and another 26 tables, similar to the 26 before, that capture the results obtained by our application for each word from the databse.

The "total" database contains the aggregated information about the corpus, each of its entry being specific to a different year and containing the total number of words, pages and volumes that were indexed by Google for that year. This table is used for normalizing the data from the other tables.

Each of the 26 tables containing the words have information referring to the number of appearances, number of pages and volumes in which the words starting with the letter specific to the table were found.

Finally, the 26 results tables contain the data about each words' cyclicity obtained using the algorithms described in the next section.

The choice of saving the words in 26 tables was done for efficiency reasons, since the application was very slow when the words were saved in a single table.

2) Services Module

This module contains the services needed for running the application (the business logic). This module contains two types of resources: on one hand, there are the services for accessing the database from the previous tier, and on the other there are implementations for the two algorithms used for identiying the words' cyclicity.

The services from the first class are responsible for the create, read, update, and delete (CRUD) operations with the "total" table, data selection for a given word, memorizing the generated graphics in the database, adding the analysis results for a given word using the two algorithms, the selection of the best results obtained, etc. Also, for all these operations is used a caching system for improving the application performances.

The second class of resources contains the implementation of the autocorrelation and the DynamicTimeWarping (DTW) algorithms. These resources receive as input the normalized graph of a given word and will output the data obtained after running each algorithm.

3) Indexer Module

This module deals with the indexing of the data from the n-grams files created by Google and, since it is responsible for the data acquisition, is the first module to be. Thus, it initially parses the files for the words starting with each letter and saves them in one of the 26 tables, and then it indexes the aggregation file for filling the "total" table.

The indexer module is also responsible for filtering the data, with the help of the WordNet lexical base, considering several criteria: the word's length should be greater than 2; the characters composing the word can only be letters, quotes, or dashes; the word cannot contain more than 3 identical consecutive characters; the word should be also present in the WordNet lexical base; information about the word's use should be present for at least 10 different years; and the dataset should contain information for at least 95% of the years in which the word was used.

The filtering's purpose is to ensure the accuracy and representativeness of the analyzed data, and thus, the words that did not respect at least one of the above criteria was removed from analysis.

The number of words that were kept for further analysis (after filtering) is presented in Table 1, along with the obtained results derived from their analysis.

4) Analyzer Module

This module is the main part of the application, being responsible for identifying the words' cyclicity. Thus, it runs the algorithms presented in the next section on the data that was saved in the database by the indexer module. It outputs the best results obtained by each of the algorithms.

First, the module iteratively selects the raw data of each word's usage. Then, this data is normalized, on a yearly base, with the help of the aggregated data from the "total" table, specifying the total number of all words' usage for each indexed year. Thus, the count of words' usage is transformed in the frequency of words' usage, having values in the [0, 1] interval. Finally, the algorithms for detecting words' cyclicity are run on this data.

To obtain the best possible results, when applying the algorithms, we varied the running parameters, which led to multiple runs of the algorithms for the same word. The algorithms have two parameters that can be adjusted: the length of the interval in which the words' cyclicity is tested and the length of the cycle.

Regarding the first parameter, for both algorithms, we varied the starting date of the interval, with a rate of 10 years, starting from 1800 and ending with 1980. Thus, for each word, we tried to detect cycles in the intervals: [1800, 2008], [1810, 2008], ... [1980, 2008].

For the second parameter, we varied the length of the cycle that we were looking for depending on the length of the interval in which words' cyclicity was tested. Thus, we varied the length of the searched cycle starting from one sixth of the whole interval and ranging up to one third of the interval. For example, for a word graph in the [1948, 2008] interval, the length of the cycle may vary between 10 ((2008-1948)/6) and 20 ((2008-1948)/3) years.

After running the two algorithms for detecting the words' cyclicity with all the presented choices for the two parameters, the best obtained results, along with the setting of the parameters that led to these results (the starting year of the analysis and the length of the cycle), were saved in the results table from the database. In Table 1, we present the best results obtained.

5) Graphical User Interface Module

The last module of the application is responsible for accessing and presenting the results of the analysis. This module is a web interface that is presented in Figure 1. It allows the selection of a given word and the visualization of its usage in time, along with the best results obtained using the two algorithms. It also shows the aggregated data, presenting general information about the dimension of the data indexed by Google and of the data retained by our application.

IV. USED ALGORITHMS

In this section, we will present the two algorithms that we used for detecting the words' cyclicity: autocorrelation and DTW.

A. Autocorrelation

Autocorrelation [8] is an analysis method for time series used for determining the correlation of a time series with its own values, shifted in time, backward and/or forward. The positive autocorrelation may be considered a special state of a persistent system in time, having the tendency to stay in the same state from one observation of the system to the next one. In practice, time series modeling geo-physics processes auto-correlate due to phenomena, such as inertia or carryover in the physical system [9].

This method may be used for identifying the signicative covariance or correlation between time-series. However, the most practical use of this analysis method is in forecasting, where it benefits from the properties of the auto-correlated time series. Since the future values of such a time series depend on the past ones, the series can be probabilistically predicted.

Having the measurements $Y = (y_1, y_2, \ldots y_N)$ for the moments in time $X = (x_1, x_2, \ldots x_N)$, where N is the total number of measurements on the time series, then the autocorrelation with the delay k (the correlation between observations separated by k years) is r_k, given by (1).

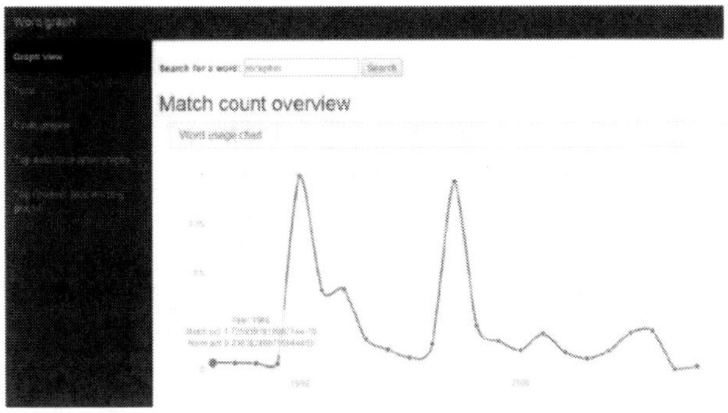

Figure 1. Example of the application output for the word rocephin.

$$r_k = \frac{\sum_{i=1}^{N-k}(y_i-\bar{y})(y_{i+k}-\bar{y})}{\sum_{i=1}^{N-k}(y_i-\bar{y})^2} \quad (1)$$

Although the sequence of moments in time when the measurements where made (X) is not explicitly used, it is assumed that the measurements where performed at equidistant moments in time.

Thus, the result of autocorrelation, the r_k coefficient, is obtained by correlating the same time series with the same values of y_i, but for different moments in time: x_i and x_{i+k}.

B. *Dynamic Time Warping (DTW)*

The DTW algorithm is well-known in many domains, being introduced in the 60s [10] and then intensely researched in the 70s in studies for voice recognition [11]. Nowadays, it is used in various domains, such as hand-writing recognition, gesture recognition, data mining and time-series clustering, computer vision, proteins alignment and chemical industry, music and signal processing, etc [12].

This algorithm earned its popularity due to its efficiency in recognizing the similarity between two time series, allowing an elastic transformation of the time series for detecting similar shapes.

Receiving at input two times series, $X = (x_1, x_2, \dots x_N)$, and $Y = (y_1, y_2, \dots y_M)$, with $M, N \in \mathbb{N}$, representing the values sequence of these time series, DTW computed the optimum solution with a complexity of O (M * N). The only restriction of this algorithm is that the series to be sampled at equidistant points in time.

In this research, we used the pseudo-code from [12] to implement the DWT algorithm for comparing some pre-defined time series with the ones obtained based on the words' usage over time. The pre-defined time series that we used had two different shapes: either sinusoidal or sinusoidal from which we maintained only the absolute values. We considered these shapes for the pre-defined time series, as these are cyclic (by definition) and thus, if a time series is similar to one of these, it means they are also cyclic. Besides varying the type of the pre-defined curves, we also varied their period, to allow the detection of cycles of various dimensions. Some examples of the used pre-defined curves can be seen in Figure 2.

V. OBTAINED RESULTS AND DISCUSSION

Some of the obtained results can be visualized in Figure 3, while in Table 1 we present the words which yielded the best scores after running the algorithms for detecting cyclic words. As it can be seen, most of these words are part of the pharmaceutical domain.

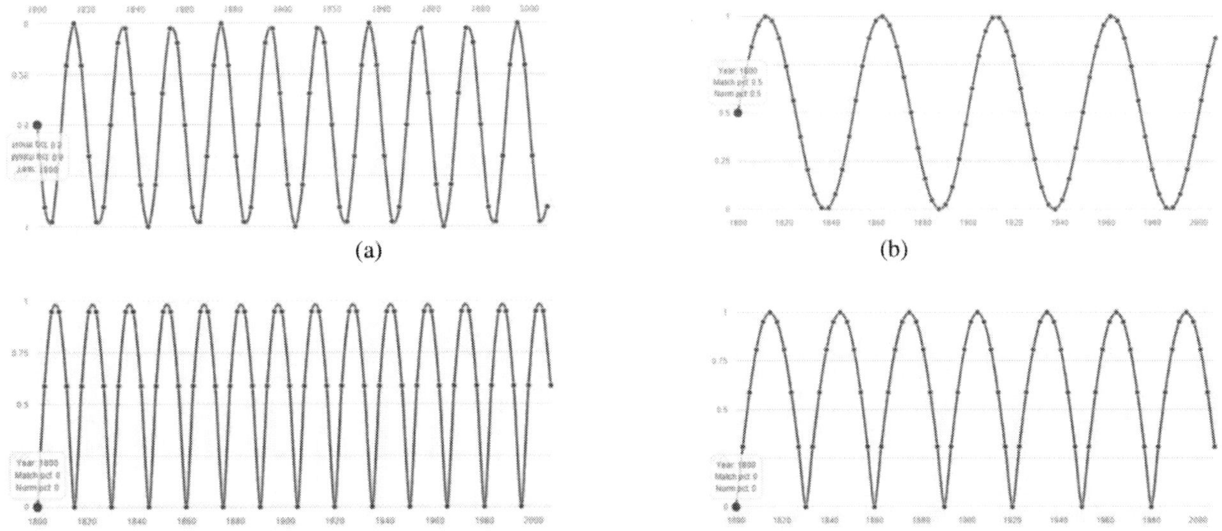

(a) (b) (c) (d)

Figure 2. Pre-defined time series used in the DTW algorithm: (a) Sinusoid with a period of 20 years; (b) Sinusoid with a period of 50 years; (c) Sinusoid using only the absolute values having a period of 30 years; (d) Sinusoid using only the absolute values having a period of 60 years.

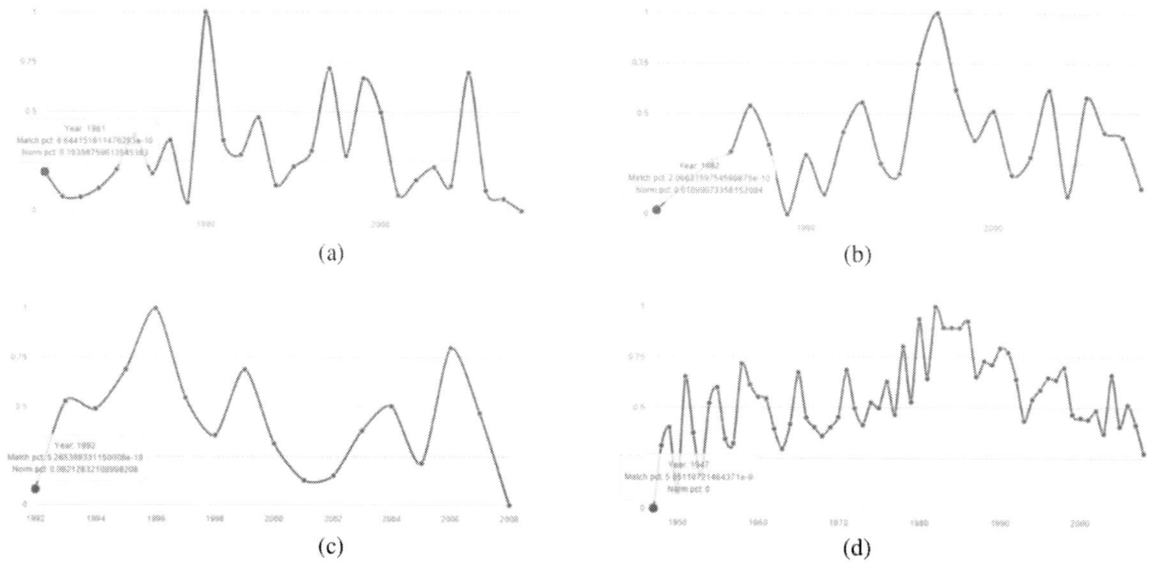

Figure 3. The normalized graph for some of the identified cyclic words (a) anaprox; (b) augmentin; (c) didanosine; (d) propylthiouracil.

TABLE I. IDENTIFIED CYCLIC WORDS

Letter	Number of analyzed words	Detected cyclic words
A	2994	abacus, abdominoplasty, agave, aircrewman, allogeneic, alphanumerical, alphavirus, anaprox, anatomical, anticipation, ape
B	2241	basuco, beatrice, belief, bland, blarney, bobbysoxer, botch, brunt, brussels, buoyancy
C	4105	capacitive, catapres, clioquinol, codex, cognac, cognizant, collision, colonization, conceding, counterinsurgency, cowherd, cushion, cyberphobia
D	2446	dadaism, dbms, deathbed, decadron, decapitated, defunct, delavirdine, deoxythymidine, desertification, desyrel, didanosine, dislocate, dissect, domesticated, dronabinol
E	1808	egotrip, egyptologist, empennage, enalapril, enclosure, enthrall, eumycota, evergreen, excrement, extensively
F	1652	fainthearted, festering, fiddler, figment, fleshiness, frisian
G	1280	geological, gifted, glassy, gulf
H	1585	haldol, helmsman, herbaceous, hermes, hillbilly, history, honeycomb, horticultural, hydroxyzine, hyena, hypervolaemia
I	1875	illegible, immersion, inderal, induct, informercial, interlace, intralinguistic
J	371	joust
L	1506	lac, legitimately, leo, lifelessness, limnodromus, lindsay, linkup, llama, lopressor, lyophilise
M	2298	manifestation, marge, mentha, metricate, microelectronic, microphone, molehill, monosyllabic, montgomery, multiethnic, munro
N	876	nadolol, naltrexone, ncdc, nelson, neosporin, nonproliferation, nureyev, nydrazid
O	952	ominous, omnipresent, onerous, opponent, optative, oswald, outlandish, outpouring, overcome, overflight
P	3474	paedophile, paintbox, paramount, paternally, pectoralis, personify, pharmacogenetics, pimpled, plantago, plentitude, plop, polygonal, popular, postindustrial, privatize, propylthiouracil, psittacosaur, pyramid
R	1918	rarely, recoverable, reluctantly, remodel, renegade, resident, resoluteness, retrovirus, reverberating, ritalin, robertson, rocephin, roleplaying, root
S	4338	saquinavir, saturate, schtik, scott, scrutinise, seats, sectarianism, sedum, serratus, shoed, soliton, speaker, sporanox, sunchoke, supporter, swiss, switchblade
T	2127	teleconference, temp, theologian, tonocard, topicalization, toradol, tracing, transparence, tranylcypromine
U	1434	underboss, unfettered, unfinished, unimpeded
V	780	vacate, velban, videodisc
W	875	waking, willis, workings
Z	101	zinacef, zovirax

After applying the two algorithms, we compared the obtained results to highlight the differences between them, as well as each ones' advantages and disadvantages. Thus, both algorithms may be used for detecting if a graph varies regularly, but there are differences in what may be considered regular. Autocorrelation offers the best results when the graph has a shape that repeats at certain intervals, without imposing any restriction on the curve's shape. DTW algorithm compares the graph with a predefined shape. Thus, it detects that the time series varies regularly only if the two shapes are alike.

Thus, autocorrelation offers results that can be more generic, while DTW offers more specific ones, being required that the analyzed graph to be similar to the one imposed for comparison. From this observation comes the main advantage of autocorrelation, but also its main disadvantage. The advantage is given by the fact that the analyzed curves may have any shape, the only requirement being to vary regularly in order to autocorrelate. However, its disadvantage is generated by the fact that the graph may also autocorrelate when it is almost constant in time, with small variation that may be seen as noise. Therefore, the words whose use frequency stabilized in time will be identified by this algorithm as cyclic, generating inaccurate results.

VI. Conclusions

In this paper, we presented a system capable of indexing the unigram dataset provided by Google and of analyzing the graph of each indexed word. The analysis was done with the help of two different algorithms, autocorrelation and DTW, to establish if the graphic representation of the words' usage in time was cyclic or not.

As it can be seen in Figure 3 and in Table 1, most of the words whose use was cyclic in time are from the pharmaceutic domain. This may be attributed to the fact that the interest for pharmaceutic products (especially for the ones present in the results) tends to be sinusoidal, with ups and downs.

Finally, based on the obtained results, we cannot say which of the two algorithms is better, both having advantages as well as disadvantages. As already mentioned, autocorrelation has the advantage of identifying if a graph is cyclic, no matter what shape it has, but may end up with false autocorrelations in the case of constant use of a word. On the other hand, DTW has the advantage that to be cyclic means to have a sinusoidal shape, and thus it uses sinusoids to compare the words' usage graphs with. However, if the graph is cyclic but does not have a sinusoidal shape, then DTW will fail to identify it as cyclic.

In the future, we aim to continue the current research by grouping the cyclic words in clusters such as events, products, personalities, locations, sentiments, actions, etc. Thus, based on the word and its category, different conclusions may be drawn. For example, for cyclic words from the events cluster, one could predict when that type of event might happen or might become popular again, based on its cyclicity.

Acknowledgment

This work has been funded by University Politehnica of Bucharest, through the "Excellence Research Grants" Program, UPB – GEX. Identifier: UPB–EXCELENȚĂ–2016 Aplicarea metodelor de învățare automată în analiza seriilor de timp (Applying machine learning techniques in time series analysis), Contract number 09/26.09.2016.

References

[1] J.-B. Michel et al., Quantitative analysis of culture using millions of digitized books. Science, 331 (6014), pp. 176-182, 2011.

[2] A. M. Petersen, J. Tenenbaum, S. Havlin, and H. E. Stanley, "Statistical Laws Governing Fluctuations in Word Use from Word Birth to Word Death," Scientific reports, 2, Article number: 313, 2012, doi:10.1038/srep00313.

[3] S. Roth, "Fashionable Functions: A Google Ngram View of Trends in Functional Differentiation (1800-2000)," Int. J. of Technology and Human Interaction, 10(2), pp. 34-58, April-June 2014, doi: 10.4018/ijthi.2014040103.

[4] A. Acerbi, V. Lampos, P. Garnett, and R. A. Bentley, The Expression of Emotions in 20th Century Books, PloS one 8, no. 3, e59030, March 20, 2013

[5] A. Islam, E. Milios, and V. Kešelj, "Comparing Word Relatedness Measures Based on Google n-grams," Proceedings of COLING 2012: Posters, pp. 495–506, December 2012

[6] D. T. Wijaya and R. Yeniterzi, "Understanding Semantic Change of Words Over Centuries," Proceedings of the 2011 international workshop on DETecting and Exploiting Cultural diversiTy on the social web, pp. 35–40, ACM, 2011.

[7] G. A. Miller, WordNet: A Lexical Database for English. Communications of the ACM, Vol. 38, No. 11, pp. 39-41, 1995.

[8] G. E. P. Box and G. M. Jenkins, Time series analysis: forecasting and control, revised ed. Holden-Day, 1976.

[9] D. Meko. Autocorrelation. GEOS 585A: Applied Time Series Analysis, Course 3, The University of Arizona, 2005 [Online, accessed June, 2017]. Retrieved from: http://shadow.eas.gatech.edu/~jean/paleo/Meko_Autocorrelation.pdf

[10] R. Bellman and R. Kalaba, "On adaptive control processes," IRE Trans. on Automatic Control, vol. 4, no. 2, pp. 1–9, 1959.

[11] C. Myers, L. Rabiner, and A. Rosenberg, "Performance tradeoffs in dynamic time warping algorithms for isolated word recognition," IEEE Transactions on Acoustics, Speech, and Signal Processing, vol. 28, no. 6, pp. 623–635, 1980.

[12] P. Senin, "Dynamic time warping algorithm review," Information and Computer Science Department University of Hawaii at Manoa Honolulu, USA, 855, 1-23, 2008.

Using Web Based Education Technologies to Develop and Teach Traditional and Distance Learning Computing Courses

Daniela Marghitu, Shubbhi Taneja, Derek Gore
Department of Computer Science and Software Engineering,
Auburn University, Auburn, Alabama, USA
Email: *daniela.marghitu,szt0024,dag0018*@auburn.edu

Abstract— **Widespread use of the Web and other Internet technologies in postsecondary education has exploded in the last 15 years. Using a set of items developed by the National Survey of Student Engagement, research studies show a general positive relationship between the use of web-based education technologies and student engagement and learning outcomes. Recent studies forecast that by 2018, 51% of Science, Technology, Engineering, and Mathematics (STEM) jobs will be in computing. Bureau of Labor Statistics 2008-2018 Employment states that 75% of the engineering jobs in the U.S. are going to be in computing. This presentation will introduce innovative Web Based Educational Learning Management Systems, Video Management systems, and Training and Assessment application successfully used at Auburn University in developing traditional and distance learning computer courses.**

Keywords - Web-based education technologies; accessibility; learning management systems (LMS).

I. Introduction

There has been a rapid infusion of technology into traditional instruction methods utilized in higher education [9] [11]. Using a set of tools developed by the National Survey of Student Engagement, research studies show a general positive relationship between the use the of Web Based Education technologies, student engagement, and learning outcomes. Recent studies forecast that by 2018, 51% of STEM jobs will be in computing [1]. Bureau of Labor Statistics 2008-2018 Employment states that 75% of all engineering jobs in the U.S. are going to be in computing, organized as shown in Figure 1 [2].

Roadmap: In Section 2, we discuss the motivations to use educational technology in web-based courses. In Section 3, we discuss the video management web-based system used by Auburn to facilitate online learning for off-campus students. In Section 4, we talk about a tool that provides our students training to learn MS Office in the most convenient manner possible. We conclude our findings and experience in Section 5.

II. Motivation for using Web-Based Education Technologies

Auburn University enables all faculty members to use the Canvas learning management system [3] hosted by Amazon Web Services cloud [4] to deliver all courses.

Canvas is fully intergraded with Banner [5] (an administrative software package and a highly-integrated web-based system with a common database that is shared by everyone who uses it). Canvas is substantially conformant with Level A and Level AA of the Web Content Accessibility Guidelines version 2.0 (WCAG 2.0) [6]. Canvas includes: lectures, assignments, practice tests, exams, grades, links to other related sites, other student resources; see Figure 2. Students and instructors have constant access to these resources.

III. Video Management Web-Based System

For distance learning courses, Ponopto [7] video management system is used to manage, live stream, record, and share videos, and is fully integrated with Canvas learning system; see Figure 3.

IV. Training and Assessment Web-Based Applications

MyITLab [8] is a personalized cloud-based application, providing high-fidelity HTML5 Office Simulations for teaching and learning digital literacy and Microsoft Office productivity.

Students have a realistic, simulated training environment that allows them to learn Microsoft Office skills. It offers help and hints that use multiple methods of completion, is automatically graded, and provides feedback so they can see what they've done incorrectly.

Instructors can easily assess their students' Word, Excel, Access, and PowerPoint skills by assigning projects that are submitted and immediately graded by MyITLab's Grader engine. The engine also captures potential integrity violations at both the document and content level to ensure students are completing their own work.

MyITLab [8] includes a road map for continued accessibility enhancements that meets WCAG 2.0. The MyITLab interface features several aids for low-vision and mobility-impaired users, including: voicing, keyboard controls, and adjustable screen settings: The *Accessibility Mode* brings up the Accessibility Toolbar, which reads MyITLab aloud, highlights text as it is read, and provides options to translate the MyITLab interface into several languages [10][11]. The new MyITLab Virtual Keyboard is designed to ensure that every student can complete the simulation activity (see Figure 4).

This keyboard allows for users with visual impairments, with non-PC hardware, such as a Mac computer, to enjoy the same user experience.

V. Conclusion and Future Work

Web Based Education Technologies are rapidly and fundamentally changing higher education, enabling students to learn what they want, when they want, and how they want. Many developing countries don't have access to Web Based Education

Institutions of higher education also have the ethical responsibility of providing learning opportunities to all. Constructive partnerships between publishing, education and assistive technology companies, academia and governmental education institutions are vital for maximizing the success, and inclusiveness of the Web Based teaching and learning.

References

[1] CEW Goergetown. Computer scienc, 2012.

[2] U.S. Bureau of Labor Statistics: http://www.bls.gov/, [Accessed March 19 2017].

[3] Canvas: https://www.canvaslms.com/, [Accessed March 19 2017].

[4] Amazon Web Service Cloud: https://aws.amazon.com/, [Accessed March 19 2017].

[5] Banner: http://www.ellucian.com/Software/Banner-Student/, [Accessed March 19 2017].

[6] Web Content Accessibility Guidliness 2.0: https://www.canvaslms.com/accessibility, [Accessed March 19 2017].

[7] Ponopto: https://www.panopto.com/, [Accessed March 19 2017].

[8] MyItLab Accessibility: http://wps.pearsoned.com/accessibility, [Accessed March 19 2017].

[9] Mull, C. A., & Sitlington, P. L. (2003). The role of technology in the transition to postsecondary education of students with learning disabilities a review of the literature. The Journal of Special Education, 37(1), 26-32

[10] Burgstahler, S. (2002). Working together: People with disabilities and computer technology. [University of Washington], DO-IT.

[11] Timmermann, S. (1998). The role of information technology in older adult learning. New Directions for Adult and Continuing Education, 1998(77), 61-71.

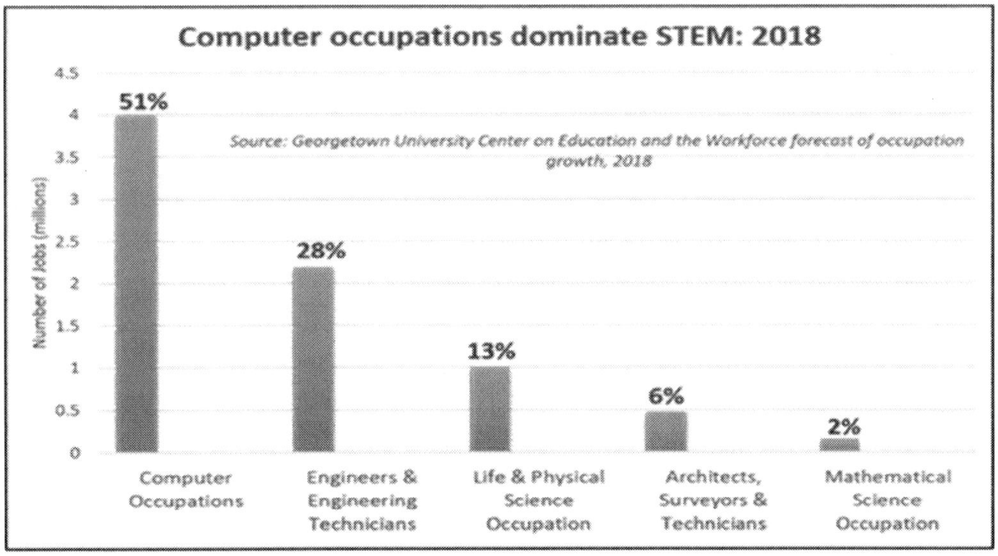

Fig.1 STEM jobs by the year 2018

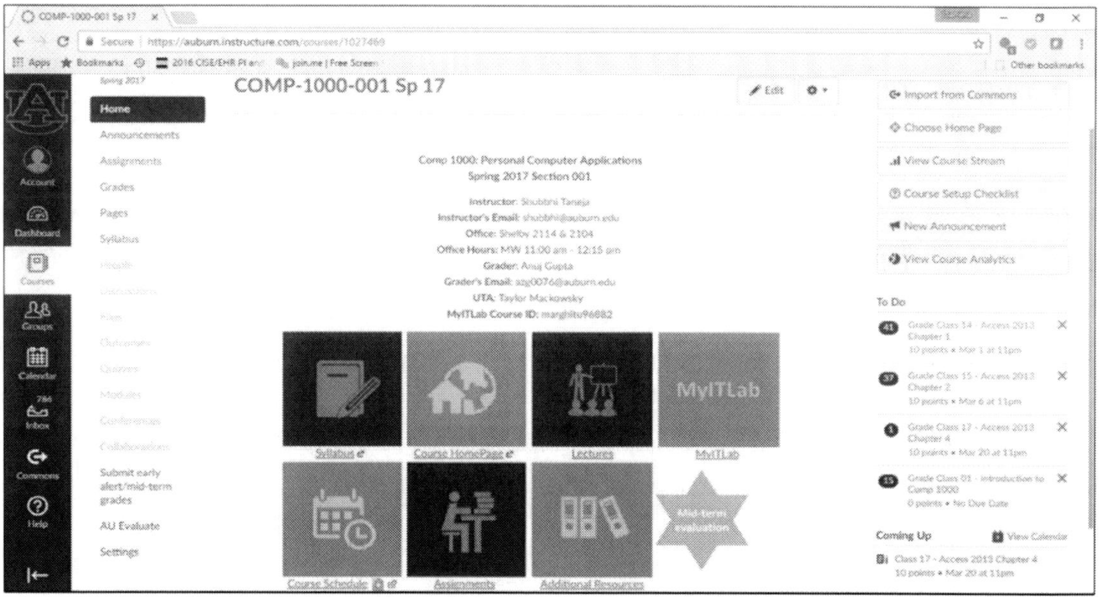

Fig.2 Canvas coures template

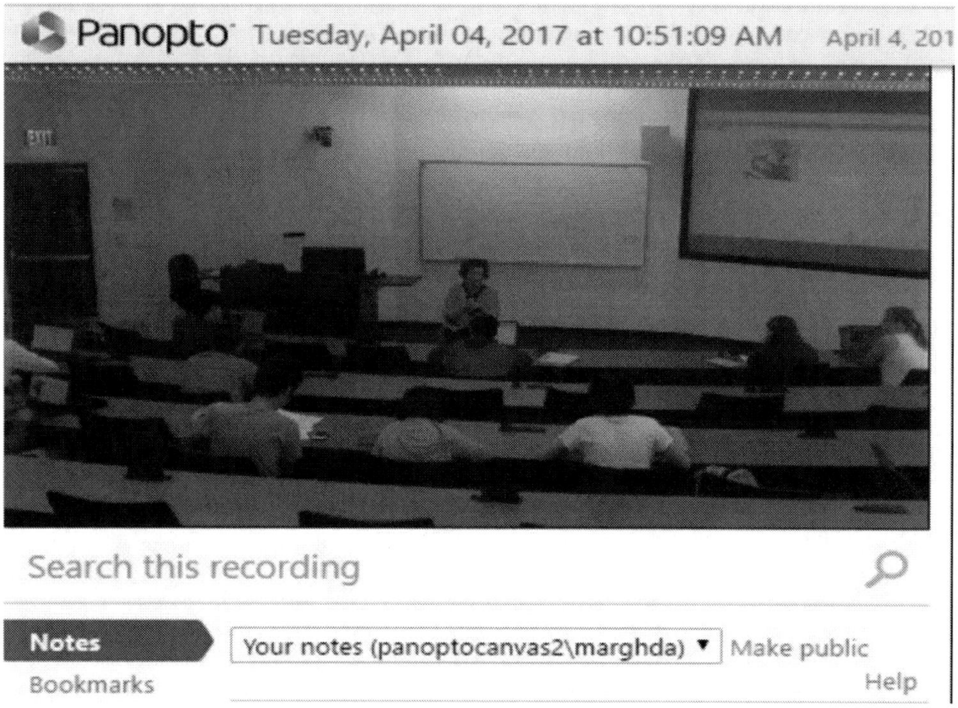

Fig.3 Ponopto recorded lectures

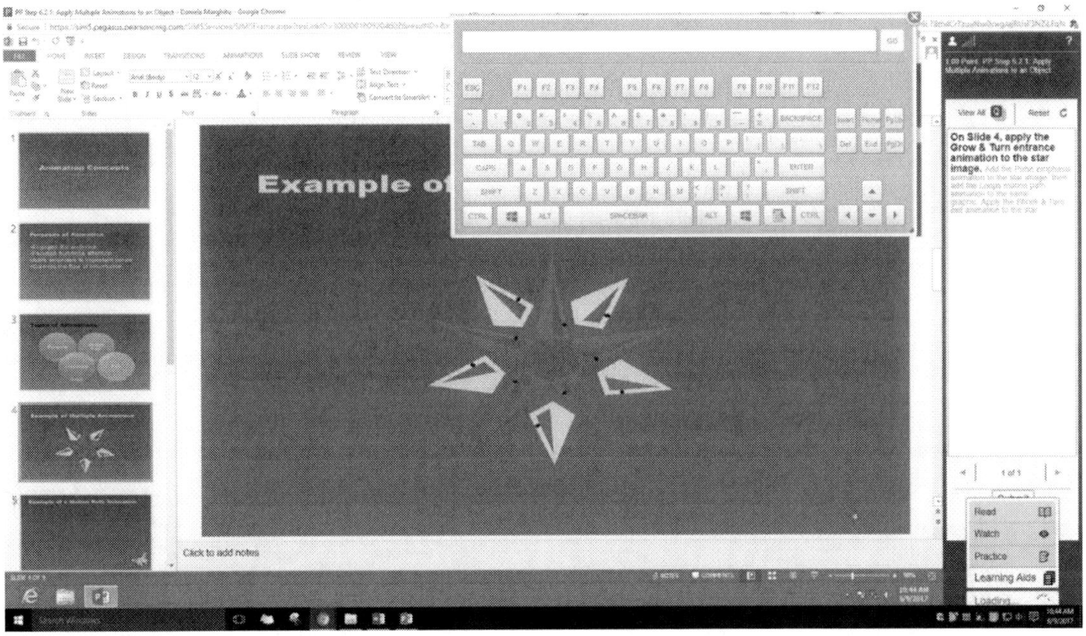

Fig.4 MyITLab student interface.

About a Decentralized 2FA Mechanism

Marc Jansen
Computer Science Institute
University of Applied Sciences Ruhr West
Bottrop, Germany
marc.jansen@hs-ruhrwest.de

Abstract— **Web based security applications have become increasingly important in the past years. Especially in times of blockchain based crypto currencies, user authentication is a critical aspect for the overall security, integrity and acceptance of such systems. While blockchain technologies provide a decentralized approach, the client side still largely relies on centralized security approaches. Those centralized approaches are easier to implement, but at the same time bear the risk of usual security flaws. Therefore, this paper presents a decentralized approach for increasing the security by adding a decentralized two-factor authentication mechanism to the execution of operations.**

Keywords—blockchain, multi-factor authentication, decentralization

I. Introduction

Usually, nowadays the security of a certain application (especially blockchain based technologies, like Bitcoin [1]) that deals with security relevant data is protected not only by single passwords but multi-factor authentication mechanisms. Here, the most prominent implementations use two-factor authentications (2FA) in which a certain user of a system has to identify himself with two components, e.g., things only the user knows, possesses or something that is inseparable from the user [2].

Here, a well accepted pattern is that a user first authenticates with his username and a corresponding password and, in a second step, the second authentication mechanism is used in order to finally authenticate the user for the task in question. In common implementations, the second step of authentication needs a central repository, e.g., a central database that stores the necessary information in order to authenticate the user.

Although two-factor authentication already increases the security of a given system, it still encounters the drawback of the centralized database storing a secret only the user who wants to authenticate knows. This database could potentially be corrupted by different means. Therefore, in this paper, we describe a decentralized approach for the implementation of a two-factor authentication mechanism that does not need a centralized repository for storing certain information necessary for user authentication. First, we describe the fundamental idea of the approach, followed by different ways of implementation, depending on different business cases and functionalities that the underlying blockchain provides.

Therefore, the following parts of the paper are organized as follows: Section 2 provides an overview about the current state of the art. Afterwards, Section 3 describes a reference architecture in order to introduce some terms in the context of this paper, followed by a description of the implementation of the approach in general terms in Section 4 in order to motivate the descriptions of the algorithms. Section 5 concludes the paper by a discussion and an outlook for future work.

II. State of the Art

Blockchain based technologies are used in a large number. While digital currencies are still, by far, the most used scenario for blockchains, other scenarios have also become more and more prominent. At the same time, security of such systems needs to be improved in order to increase the broad acceptance. Since the blockchain is in itself a decentralized approach, all other related parts should preferably also be decentralized. Recent hacks in the blockchain community have shown that there is a tremendous need for securing blockchain technologies not only by a usual username / password based approach, but, additionally, to provide at least a two-factor authentication mechanism. Preferably, all parts that are related to the security of the approach should be implemented in a decentralized way. Therefore, in general, the need for decentralized user authentication mechanism, including 2FA is given.

Looking at different approaches currently implemented based on blockchain technologies, there are already implementations far beyond simple currencies, e.g., for securing intellectual property rights, that make use of blockchain technologies, e.g., OriginStamp [3]. This is, to some extent similar, because, for a decentralized 2FA mechanism, someone has to prove that he is the only one (and therefore also the first) who knows a certain secret. Furthermore, decentralized naming service also exist already, e.g., Blockstack [4] and Namecoin [5].

Additionally, there are a couple of 2FA implementations based on the Time-based One-Time Password algorithm (TOTP) [6]. Here, a number of different clients exist that allow to easily integrate 2FA at the client side, e.g., GoogleAuthenticator [7] or 1Password [8].

An approach for 2FA authentication on the Bitcoin protocol is presented in [9]. This approach uses a two party-party signature scheme compatible with ECDSA (Elliptic Curve Digital Signature Algorithm) [10]. Here, a mobile device is used in order to provide the second authentication factor. One problem that occurs with this approach is that the mobile device that generates the second factor needs to directly communicate with the PC that generates the transaction. This is not possible in general, depending on the current network configuration especially of the PC that generates the transaction, e.g., there could be communication problems in usual NAT (Network Address Translation) networks. Therefore, another solution needs to be chosen in order to allow a general approach.

Therefore, currently, an approach does not exist that allows to have a decentralized 2FA process that does not need to store the secret centrally, as it is necessary for the TOTP implementation, for example. Therefore, in this paper, we provide such an approach, that utilizes TOTP and different other approaches (depending on the business case and the functionalities of the underlying blockchain) in order to achieve the goal of a 2FA process without the central storage of the necessary secret. At the same time, we of course ensure that the secret is only known by the user who wants to get authenticated.

III. ARCHITECTURE

The following two subsections provide an overview of some terms with respect to the architecture that are important to be clarified in order to provide access to the presented approach. On one hand, a description of the reference architecture of a modern blockchain based approach, along with corresponding terms, and on the other hand fundamental aspects of a TOTP architecture are introduced.

A. Description of the reference architecture for the presented approach

The remaining part of the section makes some assumptions related to the underlying architecture of the blockchain network and how users interact with this network. This reference architecture is shown in Figure 1.

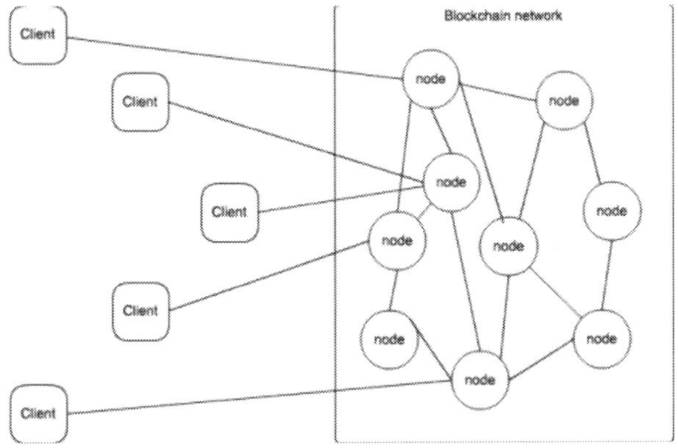

Figure 1: Reference architecture for the communication between clients and the peers of a blockchain network

As it could be seen, the clients are directly communicating with the peers of the blockchain network, which we will denote as nodes in the remaining part of the paper. It is important to state here that this reference architecture is not something special nor a limiting factor for the universality of the presented approach. It is rather a very common architecture for modern blockchain based systems.

B. Some words on a general TOTP architecture

The general idea of the TOTP protocol is that a client and an authentication provider agree on a secret. On the client side, this secret could be stored on different devices, e.g., the smartphone of the user, the tablet and/or his PC/Laptop. In order for the user to get authenticated, the agreed secret is used later on for the creation of the time based on-time password, e.g., a passwords that is only valid for a certain period of time. The general architecture for this is shown in figure 2.

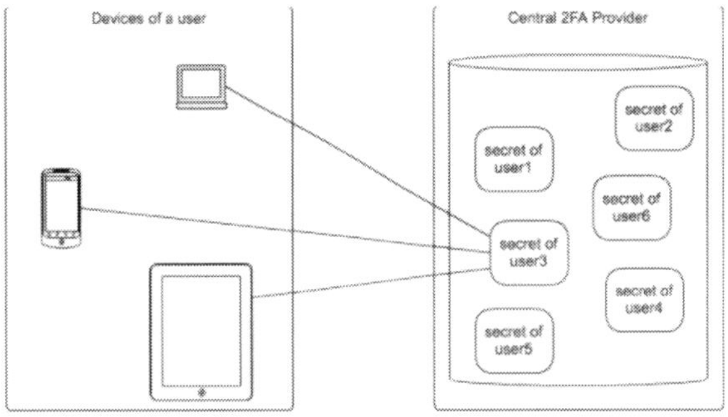

Figure 2: Architectural overview of usual TOTP implementations

Here, it is important to note that the secret shared between different devices of the user and the secret stored for that user in the centralized system are identical. At the same time, the central database is of course capable of storing secrets for other users also. As the database stores secrets for an increasing number of users, it becomes a more interesting target for potential attacker.

IV. IMPLEMENTATION

The following two subsections first describe the idea of the implementation and then the necessary algorithms for the implementation.

A. Approach

In usual 2FA implementations that make use of the TOTP protocol, the secret that is used for the creation of the one-time password is stored in some central repository. In order to overcome the necessity of the central repository, while at the same time not making the secret available to everybody, the basic idea we are following here, is to make the secret a one-time pad that is securely stored in a blockchain, allowing someone who knows the secret at a certain point in time to get authenticated towards the decentralized system. With this, in contrast with the usual TOTP implementations, not only is the generated one-time password a one-time pad as well, but also the secret that is used in order to generate the one-time password becomes a one-time pad.

Imagine a user of a certain system wants to perform a certain operation, e.g., a crypto currency transaction, then the user first needs to login to the system (by using his/her credentials). For each security related operation that the user performs in the system, the user sends the necessary information for the operation, including a TOTP based password along with the secret that is necessary in order to generate the TOTP. In order to prevent an attacker from reusing this secret and trying to get authenticated as the original user, the secret needs to be destroyed after the first usage. Additionally, by providing the secret, the user can prove that he/she already knew the secret beforehand. In order to be able to perform additional operations, also secured by the 2FA mechanism, the user has to generate a new secret with the last trusted operation he/she performed in the system, and, by this, creating a chain of trust. Here, different scenarios might be possible depending on the functionality of the underlying blockchain technology:

Scenario 1: If the underlying blockchains supports some means of attachments to an operation, the newly generated secret could be hashed and stored as an attachment to the last accepted operation.

Scenario 2: If we just have a very basic blockchain that does not allow for attachments nor sidechains or assets, the secret could be stored in the blockchain itself, secured by a Distributed Trusted Timestamp (DTT) approach [11]. Therefore, within the last trusted operation, the user generates a new secret, hashes this secret and creates a blockchain address from the hash of the secret. In order to timestamp the secret, the user transfers the minimum number of tokens to this newly created blockchain address and by this registers the secret in the system.

Scenario 3: If the underlying blockchains supports sidechains or additional assets, a security sidechain/asset could be developed in the blockchain, that stores the newly created secret. This approach also has an additional business case: Here, the security tokens could be commercialized in order to allow users to "buy" additional security (in terms of 2FA) for their operations. Basically, this implementation follows the same ideas as scenario 2 for the implementation of a DTT based approach, but without the problem of polluting the main blockchain with a large number of addresses holding just the minimal amounts of tokens, e.g., of a cryptocurrency, just for authentication, without a possibility of getting these tokens back active in the system.

Independent of which of the three scenarios are chosen, in order for the system to trust the next operation of the user, the system receives the secret sent by the user and can verify it. This verification is again a little bit different, depending on which of the above described scenarios is chosen:

Verification in scenario 1: The node that receives the operation extracts the secret of the user from the operation, hashes it and checks if the hash fits the hash of the attachment from the last accepted operation of the user.

Verification in scenarios 2 and 3: Again, the node that receives the operation extracts the secret of the user from the operation and creates the corresponding blockchain/sidechain/asset address for the hash of the secret. If the first transaction to this address came from the user who currently wants to get authenticated, the system will accept the current secret.

After accepting the secret, the node can calculate the TOTP password from the accepted secret and compare it with the TOTP password of the user that was sent within the latest operation, the system can successfully authenticate the user and accept the operation.

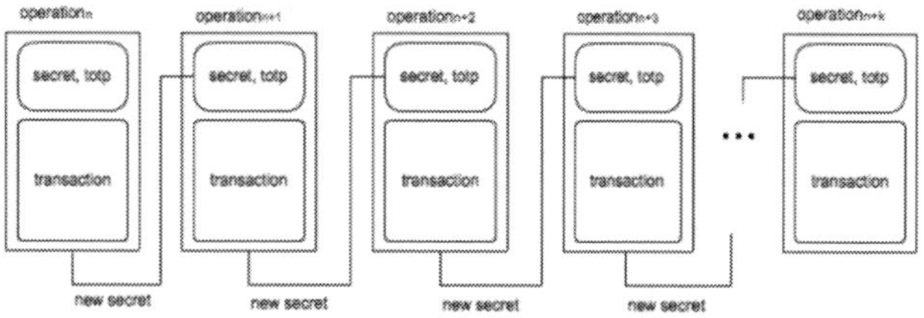

Figure 3: The chain of trust in which every last transaction creates a new secret

As shown in figure 3, by this, a chain of trust for the user will be created that allows to accept the (n+1)th-operation as long as the system has trusted the n-th operation.

B. *Algorithms*

Basically, the described approach needs two algorithms, one on the client side and one for the system that receives the operations of the client, referred to as a node in the following. First of all, the algorithm (figure 4) for the client side could be described as:

```
performOperation(transactionData) {
        totp = calculateTotp(secret)
        performCentralOperation(secret, totp,
        transactionData)
        secret = generateNewSecret()
        hashedSecret = hash(secret)
        blockchainAddress =
        generateBlockchainAddress(hashedSecret)
        transferToken(blockchainAddress)
}
```

Figure 4: Client side operation in case of scenarios 2 and 3

The following algorithm (figure 5) describes the functionality necessary on a node in order to trust the transaction sent by the client:

```
executeOperation(clientSecret, totp,
transactionData) {
        if (trust(clientSecret, totp)) {
        executeTransaction(transactionData)
        }
}

trust(clientSecret, totp) {
        hashedSecret = hash(clientSecret)
        blockchainAddress =
generateBlockchainAddress(hashedSecret)
        firstTransaction =
getFirstTransaction(blockchainAddress)

        if (firstTransation.sender.equals(client)) {
                generatedTotp = calculateTotp(secret)

                if (generatedTotp.equals(totp)) {
                        return true;
                }
        }

        return false;
}
```

Figure 5: Node operation

By this, the node can trust the client and perform the provided transaction. This trust is built not only on the asynchronously signed transaction data (that still needs to be checked by the above used `executeTransaction()` method, since it is not reflected in the above code), as usual in, e.g., blockchain technologies, but also on the second factor authentication via the TOTP protocol in a decentralized way.

V. Conclusion & Outlook

The described approach currently lacks the possibility to check that a certain secret is really only used once. In order to achieve this, the tokens transferred to the newly generated blockchain address could be interpreted as semaphores. By adding a certain functionality to the above presented algorithm 2 that sends the tokens from the address back to the original sender, the characteristic of a one-time-pad could be achieved. It is ensured that the node can actually perform this operation, since it will generate the corresponding public and private key of the blockchain address along with the generation of the address itself from the hashed secret received by the client.

Also, another drawback would be solved by the above mentioned interpretation of the tokens as semaphores: the used blockchain would not be polluted by a large number of address holding the minimal number of tokens.

Possible next steps include the implementation of the proposed approach on top of an existing blockchain technology. Here, the blockchain that is used for the DTT does not necessarily need to be the same as the blockchain that the operations are performed on. Furthermore, a detailled discussion about possible drawbacks of the presented approach are necessary.

References

[1] S. Nakamoto, "Bitcoin: A Peer-to-Peer Electronic Cash System", https://Bitcoin.org/Bitcoin.pdf, last visited: 28.11.2016

[2] "How to extract data from an iCloud account with two-factor authentication activated". iphonebackupextractor.com. Retrieved 2016-06-08.

[3] https://www.originstamp.org, last visited: 08th of June 2017

[4] https://www.blockstack.org, last visited: 08th of June 2017

[5] https://www.namecoin.info, last visited: 08th of June 2017

[6] "RFC 6238 - TOTP: Time-Based One-Time Password Algorithm". Retrieved July 04, 2016.

[7] https://play.google.com/store/apps/details?id=com.google.android.apps.authenticator2&hl=de, last visited: 08th of June 2017

[8] https://1password.com, last visited: 08th of June 2017

[9] C. Mann, D. Loebenberger, "Two-factor authentication for the Bitcoin protocol. In: International Journal of Information Security", 2016, p. 1--14", doi: 10.1007/s10207-016-0325-1

[10] J. López, R. Dahab, "An Overview of Elliptic Curve Cryptography," Technical Report IC-00-10, State University of Campinas, 2000.

[11] B. Gipp, N. Meuschke, A. Gernandt, "Decentralized trusted timestamping using the crypto currency Bitcoin", Proceedings of iConference 2015, 2015.

Increasing Security of Nodes of a Blockchain by Simple Web Application Firewalls

Marc Jansen
Computer Science Institute
University of Applied Sciences Ruhr West
marc.jansen@hs-ruhrwest.de

Abstract— **In recent times, a lot of attacks against central server infrastructures have been recognized. Those infrastructures have seen attacks ranging from attacks against Internt of Things (IoT) infrastructures, via attacks against public infrastructure to attacks against cryptocurrency exchanges and blockchain based infrastructures themselves, e.g., the already almost legendary Decentralized Autonomous Organization (DAO) hack. Measured by press coverage, attacks against cryptocurrency exchanges and infrastructures seem to be among the most prominently reported attacks, probably due to the large amount of money that is stolen during those attacks and the great (but obviously still quite risky) potential (and financial involvement) of the blockchain technology. Naturally, attacks like the ones we have seen recently increase the notion of uncertainty of blockchain technologies among the people, reflected in lower values of cryptocurrencies in general. Obviously, this demands for an overall increase of security of cryptocurrency based technologies. Therefore, this paper provides an architectural approach, based on a proxy, to increase security of publicly available nodes of a blockchain based technology. Furthermore, it provides a first evaluation of the approach based on the results of an extensive community test of a new cryptocurrency.**

Keywords—blockchain; security; Web application firewall; proxy

I. INTRODUCTION

When Satoshi Nakamoto published his famous paper about a potential peer-to-peer payment system [1], the overall success of the proposed system could hardly be estimated. In 2016, bitcoin itself is dominating the cryptocurrency world by a market cap of about 12 billion $, while the overall market cap of cryptocurrencies is about 14 billion. Already those figures demand for a high security of blockchain based installations and scenarios. Blockchains are a general approach that allows to store transactional data in an audit proved way. Furthermore, there are a number of approaches that utilize blockchain technology beyond the usage of cryptocurrencies, among others, e.g., for securing intellectual property rights [2].

Nevertheless, cryptocurrencies and blockchain based technologies in general have not been widely accepted by users. Even those users already working and investing in blockchains seem to be quite suspicious, e.g., the Ethererum blockchain lost about 25% of its market cap right after the hack of the DAO platform[1]. This also supports the demand for an increase in the security of blockchain based solutions, while at the same time, blockchain based solutions provide quite easy entry points via publicly available API's in form ReST-ful Web Services [4].

In order to provide a reasonable description of the presented approach, two terms from the domain of IT-Service Management need to be introduced here, in order to properly understand what the approach allows to do and what its (natural) barriers are. Traditionally, security flaws in distributed systems could be referred to as issues. In IT-Service Management issues are further differentiated into incidents and problems. In the IT Infrastructure Library (ITIL) framework, an incident is defined as "An unplanned interruption to an IT service or reduction in the quality of an IT service." [5], while furthermore, a problem is described as "The unknown root cause of one or more existing or potential incidents." [5]. The approach described in this paper will, according to those definitions, mostly tackle incidents and it does not try to solve the underlying problems.

The remainder of this paper is organized as follows: First, an overview of the current state of the art in the domain of securing Web applications is provided. Afterwards, the architecture developed in order to control and increase the security of blockchain based applications is described, followed by a description of the implementation done for an example blockchain, the Waves Platform. Waves provides a relatively new blockchain based technology, that allows to easily create one's own tokens. It is based on the Scorex framework, developed especially for research purposes in the blockchain domain. Additionally, an evaluation of the developed approach is presented. Finally, this paper concludes with a section that provides an outlook on future work.

II. STATE OF THE ART

A number of projects currently concentrate on the security of Web based applications. First of all, the Open Web Application Security Project (OWASP) [6] needs to be mentioned here. This project continously scans the Web for traditional and new attack vectors in order to provide a list of prominent attack vectors, even ranked by their appearance. Furthermore, the project also provides schemes and patterns for the recognized attack vectors that allow to identify malicious request and to filter those malicious requests out before they actually hit the target. Prominent examples of such attack vectors are SQL (Structured Querying Language) injections, directory traversal attacks, XSS (Cross-Site-Scripting) and/or CSRF (Cross-Site-Request-Forgery)' attacks.

In order to provide security against identified attack vectors, different architectural approaches like WAFs (Web Application Firewalls) or proxy technologies are usually deployed. Here, e.g., NGINX as a lightweight Web Service instance has made its name in the community for being an easy to configure proxy that allows some basic filtering

[1] http://www.coindesk.com/understanding-dao-hack-journalists/

functionality for fiddling with attack vectors as mentioned above.

A proper proxy configuration, as necessary, e.g., for NGINX, is not easy to achieve and does not provide enough flexibility to actually filter with more specialized configurations, e.g., depending on the source of the request in connection with the target endpoint. Furthermore, it does not provide rich functionalities that allow to handle possibly recognized attacks, e.g., by blocking the attacking host for a given period of time.

Additionally, using a simple WAF does also not allow filtering the access to certain Web Service endpoints in relation to the source address of a given request.

Therefore, in order to overcome the shortcomings of the mentioned approaches, this paper provides an approach that allows both, filtering access to certain endpoints, e.g., by source address, and (at the same time) allowing to also filter for known and well documented attack vectors.

III. Architecture

In order to understand the architectural improvements implemented by the presented approach, we first have to have a look at the standard architecture of modern blockchain based implementations. Figure 1 presents an overview of an usual blockchain based architecture, consisting of an usual Peer-to-Peer (P2P) based blockchain architecture on the right-hand side in which the different nodes that participate in the network are connected with each other. On the left hand-side, the connection of a number of different clients to the nodes of the blockchain are visualized. In the upper part of the figure, a zoom to one node is presented, showing that each node actually provides two different ports to the network, one for the connection to the other nodes in the P2P network and one mainly for the connection of clients. While the port for the connection to the P2P network usually communicates over internal protocols, mostly proprietary to the blockchain, the port for the connection to the clients usually provides a ReSTful interface for the communication with the clients.

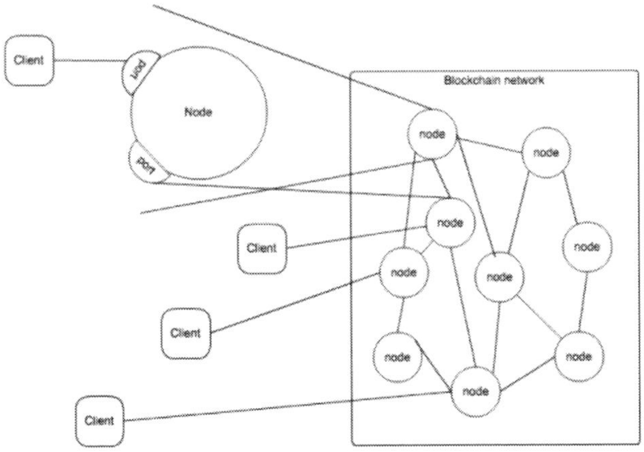

Figure 1: Basic blockchain architecture

It is important to understand that Waves uses a PoS (Proof-of-Stake) based approach, providing significant advantages above PoW (Proof-of-Work) based approaches like Bitcoin [7], especially with respect to power consumption and network fairness.

The presented approach now tackles the problem that a malicious client could try to make use of the Web Service endpoints of the node in order to enter malicious code or try to exploit issues in the node. Therefore, a proxy (according to the proxy or façade design pattern [8]) instance could be installed in front of the port for the communication with the clients in order for being able to filter against certain patterns of malicious code or restrict the access to a limited number of Web Service endpoints, e.g., necessary for the administration of the node. Figure 2 provides an overview of a node that is secured by a proxy instance.

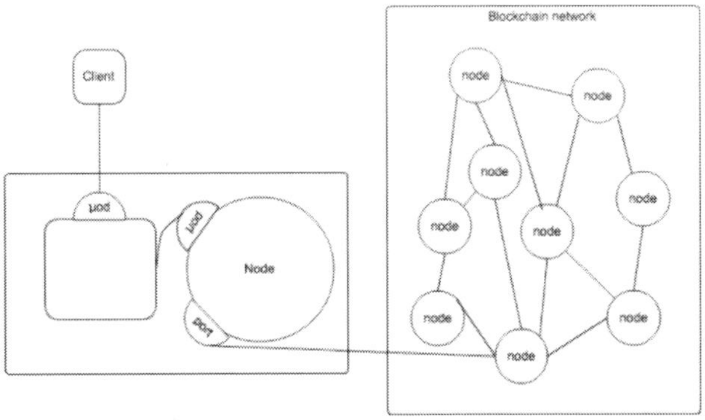

Figure 2: Architecture after the inclusion of the proxy

Internally, the proxy basically performs two different tasks. On one hand, it filters the access for different endpoints and decides if the request to a certain endpoint should be allowed or forbidden, potentially also by taking the source address of the request into account. As an additional task, the proxy could also filter for malicious code inside the request. Together, the internal architecture of the proxy could be visualized as in figure 3.

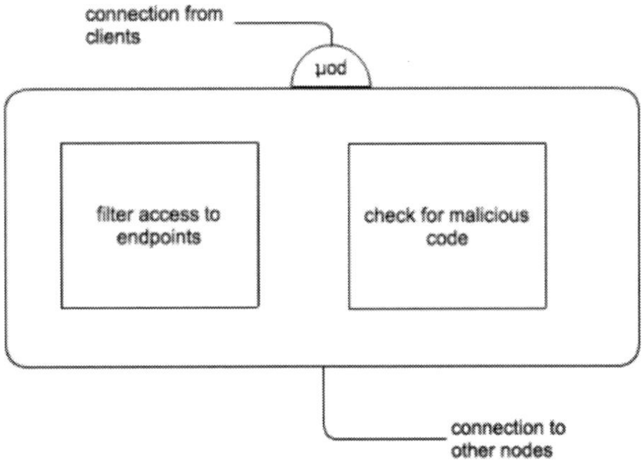

Figure 3: Internal architecture of the proxy

IV. Implementation

The description of the implementation first provides changes necessary to the usual configuration of a node of the blockchain, followed by a description of the implementation of the implementation of the proxy.

A. Configuration of the blockchain nodes

In order to implement the above described architecture efficiently, some configurations on the side of the node are necessary. First of all, it needs to be ensured that the node just listens for local connections. This could usually be achieved by different means, depending on the possibilities provided by the node. With some technologies, the nodes may just be configured (via a configuration file) to listen just to the loopback interface, other node technologies might provide something like a whitelist for addresses that are allowed to connect to the node. Also, a combination of both approaches might be possible. Furthermore, it is often helpful to change the default port of the node to a different port in order to allow the proxy to bind on the default port, and, by this, to allow the node to be reachable for the clients via the standard nodes port.

B. Implementation of the proxy

The first example implementation was based on NodeJS as a server side JavaScript framework. Although any other server side programming language and environment would also be suitable, NodeJS seemed to be a quite natural choice due powerful APIs (e.g., ExpressJS [9]) for Web based solutions. Furthermore, a couple of Web Application Firewall frameworks already exist that implement the latest findings from OWASP. Therefore, the decision was made to rely on those frameworks in order to capture standard attacks like CSRF (Cross Site Request Forgery) [10], XSS (Cross Site Scripting) [11] and alike. Also, other attacks that are not necessarily possible against a blockchain node, e.g., SQL injection or directory traversal is reasonable to check in order to take countermeasures against attackers that just randomly scan networks and try to apply random attacks. Also, Web Applications Firewall usually provide certain countermeasures against attack, e.g., by putting the address of a malicious attacker on a blacklist so that further attempts of attacks are no longer possible from listed addresses. Prominent examples for these kinds of Web Application Firewall APIs that are available for the ExpressJS Web framework are ExpressWAF [12] and/or lusca [13].

In addition to the filtering for standard attacks, also filtering for specific endpoints should be possible. For this, an easy to describe JSON based configuration file allows to configure the endpoints that are allowed to access, the source address that is allowed to access the endpoint (if defined, otherwise the endpoint is openly available) and the type of HTTP request allowed to those endpoints. The following JSON file shows an example for the configuration file.

```
[
    {
        "method": "GET",
        "source": "134.91.",
        "path": "/blocks/height"
    },
    {
        "method": "GET",
        "path": "/node/version"
    }
]
```

Here, the first entry describes that the */blocks/height* endpoint is accessible from IPs in the *134.91.0.0/16* network via HTTP GET requests, while the second entry permits HTTP GET requests to the */node/version* endpoint globally.

This configuration file is parsed in at startup of the Web Application Firewall, configures itself properly and instantiates a filter method as follows:

```
var filter = function(req, res) {
    var path = req.url;
    var source = req.connection.remoteAddress;
    var method = req.method;

    filterConfig.forEach(function(filter) {
        if (source.startsWith(filter.source) &&
            path.startsWith(filter.path) &&
            filter.method === method) {
                return true;
        }
    });

    return false;
};
```

This method was integrated in the express-http-proxy module, and by this enables the proper filtering according to the rules defined in the JSON configuration file.

V. EVALUATION

In order to evaluate if the presented approach provides an added value in the sense of increased security, the approach was implemented for securing Nodes of the Waves Platform network.

A. Scenario description

The Waves network is a relatively new blockchain that was launched in the first quarter of 2016, having an easy to use token creation process in mind. The Initial Coin Offering (ICO) started in March 2016, ending by collecting about 30.000 Bitcoin, making it the sixth ever most successful crowdfunding campaign. After this successful ICO, the team provided the code for running nodes of the network, so that investors and other interested parties could participate in stabilizing the network. At the same time, especially investors have been very concerned by the question of the security of the nodes and because of that, the Waves Platform team announced a hackathon for finding bugs in the system. This led to a tremendous effort of the community for finding bugs and reporting those via GitHub [14] to the development team.

Therefore, this github repository provides a rich resource for evaluations.

B. *Analysis*

The major idea for the evaluation presented here is to evaluate the presented approach with respect to the reported issues.

In total, 54 issues have been identified and been documented in the issues section of the Waves platform github account. These are divided into 39 issues directly in the Waves Platform software and 15 issues in the underlying Scorex framework, used by the Waves Platform developers. From these 54 issues, 19 (13 in the Waves code, 6 in Scorex code) have been security related. From those 19 reported security related issues, 11 could have been solved by using the presented approach. It is important to stress here, that in IT-Service Management terms, not the underlying problem would have been resolved, but the incident of potential execution of malicious code would have disabled. Overall, this results in 57.89% of potential attacks that would have been prevented.

The low amount of reported security related issues mainly comes from the short testing period, which seemed to be appropriate due to the fact that the underlying framework was already well tested. Later evaluations can rely on larger samples.

Having a closer look, a major difference between issues found in the underlying Scorex framework and issues in the Waves Platform code become obvious. From the 6 identified issues in the underlying Scores framework, only two would have been prevented by the usage of the presented approach, resulting in 33% of potential attacks that would have been prevented. Having a look at the Waves Platform code on top of the Scorex Framework, from the 13 identified issues, 9 would have been resolved by using the presented approach, calculating to a prevention of 69.23% of possible attacks. This clearly significant difference leads to the hypothesis that issues in more basic functionalities are harder to prevent by the presented approach than issues providing more abstract functionalities.

VI. CONCLUSION & OUTLOOK

The paper presented an architectural approach for increasing the security of peer-to-peer nodes of a blockchain technology where the functionality of the nodes is at least partially made available via Web Service endpoints. Those functionalities could be made available in a more secure way by providing a simple Web Application Firewall, allowing for filtering the access to certain endpoints by different aspects. As a result, it was shown that a large number of problems at higher level of abstraction could be eliminated by the approach, whereas the security of lower level functionalites could not be improved that dramatically.

Therefore, in future work, a possible aspect could be to also improve security of lower level functionalities by implementing a similar architectural approach directly on the protocol level of the peer-to-peer protocol in addition to the security increase on the higher-level Web Service endpoints. By this, similar results should also be achievable as for the Web Service endpoints. This, of course, needs to be evaluated in more detail. Another goal would be to integrate the described approach directly in the nodes in order to ensure that the security measures are taken by all nodes of the network and to decrease architectural complexity.

REFERENCES

[1] S. Nakamoto, "Bitcoin: A Peer-to-Peer Electronic Cash System. https://bitcoin.org/bitcoin.pdf", last visited: 28.11.2016

[2] B. Gipp, N. Meuschke, and A. Gernandt, "Decentralized Trusted Timestamping using the Crypto Currency Bitcoin", in Proceedings of the iConference 2015, Newport Beach, California, 2015.

[3] http://www.coindesk.com/understanding-dao-hack-journalists/, last visited 15th of June, 2017

[4] R. Fielding, "Architectural Styles and the Design of Network-based Software Architectures". http://www.ics.uci.edu/~fielding/pubs/dissertation/top.htm, last visited: 01.12.2016

[5] ITIL Service Strategy, "Office of Government Commerce", TSO, London, 2007.

[6] https://www.owasp.org/index.php/Main_Page, last visited 15th of June, 2017

[7] E. Gamma, R. Helm, R. Johnson, J. Vlissides, "Design Pattern – Elements of Reusable Object-Oriented Software", pp. 185-195, Addison-Wesley, 1999.

[8] https://bitcoin.org/bitcoin.pdf, last visited 15th of June, 2017

[9] https://www.owasp.org/index.php/CrossSite_Request_Forgery_(CSRF), last visited 15th of June, 2017

[10] https://www.owasp.org/index.php/Cross-site_Scripting_(XSS), last visited 15th of June, 2017

[11] http://expressjs.com, last visited 15th of June, 2017

[12] https://github.com/ToMMApps/express-waf, last visited 15th of June, 2017

[13] https://github.com/krakenjs/lusca, last visited 15th of June, 2017

[14] http://www.github.com, last visited 15th of June, 2017

Factors Affecting the Adoption of B2C by Manufacturing Companies

Pedro Lorca, Javier de Andrés, Julita García-Diez
Department of Accounting
University or Oviedo
Oviedo, Spain
e-mail: plorca@uniovi.es, jdandres@uniovi.es, julita@uniovi.es

***Abstract*— The adoption of e-commerce by Spanish companies has grown considerably in recent years. Nevertheless, it is still far from reaching the levels of other European countries, hence the interest in knowing the main features of the Spanish companies that have adopted e-commerce. We used the data from the Spanish Survey on Business Strategies, and we considered 13 variables from the Technology-Organization-Environment (TOE) model. The temporal scope of the study covers the period 2001-2013 and includes 1,770 Spanish manufacturing firms and 14,029 firm-year observations. The results show that the introduction of e-commerce is conditioned by the technological, organizational and environmental contexts. The oldest and largest companies are more prone to the implementation of e-commerce. These firms have more experience, which allows them to cope with the uncertainty implied in an innovation process. Consequently, policy measures should be aimed at reducing such uncertainty.**

Keywords—B2C; technology adoption; e-commerce; manufacturing firm.

I. Introduction

Information and communications technology (ICT) has strongly changed the relationship between companies and their customers. The enormous progress of technology together with the rapid growth of the Internet are key drivers to the exponential increase of e-commerce. In Spain, e-commerce sales exceeded 20,000 million Euros in 2015, with annual growth rates above 25% [1]. In 2006, only 8.02% of Spanish companies made online sales, ten years later this figure has grown to 20.14% [2]. Nevertheless, these figures are still far from those of other European countries, where e-commerce is much more popular.

The unequal diffusion of e-commerce has traditionally been explained by environmental, demographic, economic, technological, cultural and legal factors [3]. Previous literature confirms the impact of culture and other social determinants in the implementation of e-commerce [4][5]. Therefore, it is necessary for each country to identify the factors that help organizations to implement this kind of transactions.

In this paper, we analyze the factors that affect the introduction of Business-to-Consumer (B2C) by Spanish manufacturing companies. The identification of these factors is very useful as a preliminary step to be able to face the difficulties inherent in its adoption.

The following section contains a review of the previous literature on the implementation of e-commerce, which serves as a support for the formulation of the research hypotheses. The third section develops the empirical study with the purpose of contrasting the previous hypotheses. The sample used is taken from the Business Strategies Survey (ESEE) and covers a 13-year period. Section 4 shows the results obtained. Finally, Section 5 lays out the main conclusions of this study.

II. Theoretical Framework

There are many theoretical frameworks in the literature about the diffusion and adoption of innovations. In this paper, we focus on the factors that influence the implementation of e-commerce by Spanish manufacturing companies and we opted for the Technology-Organization-Environment (TOE) framework, since it pinpoints the perspective of the firm.

Tornatzky and Fleischer [6] developed the TOE framework to explain the factors that influence the behavior of organizations in the process of adoption and subsequent propagation of an innovation [7]. The TOE framework assumes that the adoption process within firms is effectively established through the right match between firm's internal and external factors [8]. However, the TOE framework does not offer a concrete set of factors that affect technology adoption, as it provides taxonomies of factors within their respective context where the adoption process takes place [9][10]. It contemplates three aspects of a firm's context that influence the application of technological innovations: the technological context, the organizational context and the environmental context.

The TOE framework has been used by several authors to identify factors with incidence in e-business implementation [11]-[14]. Once the three contexts are reviewed, the corresponding hypotheses are formulated.

A. Technological context

The technological context focuses on how structure and technological practices can influence the e-commerce adoption process. It includes relevant technology for the company, both external and internal. The external technological context is different between countries, but very similar within each country. For example, from the technological point of view and dealing with e-commerce, the support of the law, data security and privacy, the ways to address cybercrime concern and online business integrating capabilities contribute to the expansion of e-commerce [15] and they are the same for a geographical environment. This is why the present paper is more focused in internal technology. In particular, the following factors are considered to be relevant: website availability, investment in computer equipment, R&D intensity and the existence of previous experience in online purchase.

The availability of a website in the enterprise interested in offering e-commerce to the customers constitutes an essential issue. In the case of ICT, the development of well-structured websites leads to an improvement in the visibility of the company and in the attraction of new customers. Some authors [16] evidence the importance of website quality for the success of e-commerce. Hence, the first hypothesis is proposed in the following terms:

H_{1a}: Firms with their own website are more prone to the implementation of B2C e-commerce.

E-commerce implementation requires computer and technological resources. For example, bar code systems, automatic inventory replenishment systems, electronic funds transfer systems, electronic internet sales interfaces or integrated back office storage. This is why the availability of these resources facilitates the e-commerce implementation [17]. Therefore, we formulate the following hypothesis:

H_{1b}: Firms with greater investment in computer equipment are more prone to the implementation of B2C e-commerce.

There is a circular relationship between R&D investments and profitability. Investment in knowledge and in R&D may expand the technological opportunities; the increased knowledge endowment in turn enhances the profitability of entrepreneurial activity by facilitating recognition and exploitation of new business opportunities [18] as, for example, e-commerce. Therefore, innovative companies have more chances of success in online business. Hence, we hypothesize that:

H_{1c}: Firms with a greater effort in R&D activities are more prone to the implementation of B2C e-commerce.

Trust is a key pillar in e-commerce. Uncertainty is both one of the most important inhibitory factors when deciding its implementation, and a source of difficulties for companies with their e-commerce initiatives [19]. So, it is necessary for firms to reduce the uncertainty associated with the introduction of e-business. Therefore, previous experience in e-commerce activities as a buyer can be a positive factor for the B2C implementation. Hence, the following hypothesis is formulated:

H_{1d}: Firms with previous experience in purchasing through the internet are more prone to the implementation of B2C e-commerce.

B. *Organizational context*

The organizational context includes attributes of the firm that can facilitate or limit the adoption of innovations. After reviewing the literature, the most relevant factors of the organizational context were considered: size, previous experience, separation between ownership and control, product diversification, internationalization, operating margin and foreign capital.

The size of the enterprise is an explanatory variable widely used for several motives. First, the risk of failure is greater in small and medium-sized enterprises than in large enterprises [20]. Secondly, larger companies are able to allocate more resources and capital to face the expenses involved in the adoption [21]. Thirdly, larger firms are able to reduce the adoption costs through economies of scale [22]. Therefore, a number of prior papers evidenced the positive relationship between firm size and the adoption of e-commerce [23][24]. However, other studies do not observe such a relationship [25][26]. The reason may be that, unlike other ICT applications, e-commerce could not require large investments, making it accessible even for small and medium-sized enterprises. In the present paper, the arguments in favor of the first relationship are considered more important, so the following hypothesis is formulated:

H_{2a}: Big firms are more prone to the implementation of B2C e-commerce.

As time goes by, firms are able to accumulate resources, managerial knowledge and the ability to handle uncertainty [27]. In addition, mature firms enhance their reputation and position in the market [28]. Finally, there is evidence about the positive effect of firm age on innovative outcomes [29]. Hence, we hypothesize that:

H_{2b}: Oldest firms are more prone to the implementation of B2C e-commerce.

Another key factor in the e-commerce adoption is the top management support. The managers' commitment has positive effects throughout the organization, since it allows acquiring greater awareness of the advantages of technology, reinforces the links with the infrastructure required for its implementation and facilitates the training necessary for the use of the technology [30]. Therefore, to the extent that management is professionalized, the commitment with the implementation of e-commerce could be strengthened. Hence, the following hypothesis is formulated:

H_{2c}: Firms with separation of ownership and control are more prone to the implementation of B2C e-commerce.

Companies that make less diversified products rely on economies of scale to minimize their costs. Therefore, they seek to sell large volumes of products to a small number of customers. On the other hand, firms with a greater diversification of products try to reach a large number of customers, so e-commerce is considered a very suitable strategy for them. Hence, the following hypothesis is formulated:

H_{2d}: Firms with greater product diversification are more prone to the implementation of B2C e-commerce.

Another variable that may influence the e-commerce implementation is whether the firm develops its activity in international markets or not. The empirical literature on technological innovations shows a positive relationship between exports and innovation [31], because internationalization implies growth in competitiveness and market size. ICT reduce the impact of geographical locations and distances [32]. E-commerce offers companies a new way of reaching consumers without physical establishments, so it has been recognized as an important facilitator of international expansion [33]. Hence, we hypothesize that:

H_{2e}: The most internationalized firms are more prone to the implementation of B2C e-commerce.

The link between profitability and adoption of new technologies has been studied in the literature. Higher-performing firms are more likely to adopt ICT because of their greater availability of resources. For example, some authors [34] conclude that high-performing banks adopt product and process innovations more regularly than low-performing banks. For this reason, in the case of e-commerce, the following hypothesis is formulated:

H_{2f}: Firms with high profitability are more prone to the implementation of B2C e-commerce.

Most of the reasons cited in the literature support a positive relationship between multinational ownership and ICT adoption. This is because firms forming part of a group are able to reduce the risk involved in the adoption of new technologies [35]. The existence of an external network plays a substantial role in the adoption process, since networking heightens the awareness of the innovation and increases the likelihood of its adoption [36]. The literature has found empirical evidence to support this positive relationship [32]. Therefore, the hypothesis formulated is:

H_{2g}: Firms with greater presence of foreign capital are more prone to the implementation of B2C e-commerce.

C. *Environmental context*

The environmental context is based on the fact that the company is surrounded by multiple stakeholders (customers, suppliers, competitors, government, financial institutions, society and many more), that have decisive influence, among other aspects, on the need to innovate, the ability to obtain resources for innovation and the ability to make the most of them [6]. Regarding ICT implementation, the environment within which the firm performs its activities and the pressure of the stakeholders play an important role [11][37]. The environmental factor has also been called the institutional factor [14] or external pressure [38]. The Institutional Theory [39] points out the influence of environmental variables in companies' decisions, one of them being whether to implement e-commerce.

In the present paper, one variable regarding the environment of the firm is considered; it is customer concentration.

The greater the number of customers, the greater the advantages of implementing e-commerce, since the fixed costs caused by its implementation could be distributed among more users. In addition, online business allows to reach a greater number of potential customers. Hence, we hypothesize that:

H_{3a}: Firms with greater number of customers are more prone to the implementation of B2C e-commerce.

Finally, industry in which the firm operates may have an important influence on the e-commerce adoption. This variable reflects business environment factors, such as heterogeneity and uncertainty. Firms in different industries have to deal with different types of business environment dynamics, which may affect e-commerce adoption [40]. The strategic value of e-commerce seems to be different depending on the sector. That is to say, it becomes a competitive necessity in those industries where competition is very aggressive and competitors are making intensive use of it [41]. Therefore, in this paper the industry ascription was used as a control variable.

The proposed model is shown graphically in Figure 1.

III. EMPIRICAL STUDY

To contrast the formulated hypotheses, an empirical analysis is carried out on a sample of Spanish manufacturing companies. This section exposes the formation of the database, the variables used, the main descriptive statistics of the sample and the methodology used for hypotheses testing.

A. *Database*

To carry out the empirical study we used the Survey on Business Strategies (Encuesta sobre Estrategias Empresariales - ESEE), elaborated by the Spanish Ministry of Science and Technology. This survey is one of the most representative databases of Spanish companies, since ESEE is a reliable source for information on the strategies of Spanish companies. The reference population of the ESEE is constituted by the Spanish manufacturing companies with 10 or more employees.

In the present study, the period between 2001 and 2013 was taken as temporal scope. After eliminating the companies for which information was not available, we formed a database comprising 1,770 companies.

B. *Variables in the analysis*

Taking into account the theoretical development and the hypotheses formulation, we considered a number of variables for our analysis. These variables are displayed in Table I. Moreover, twenty dummy variables were considered for the industry in which firm operates.

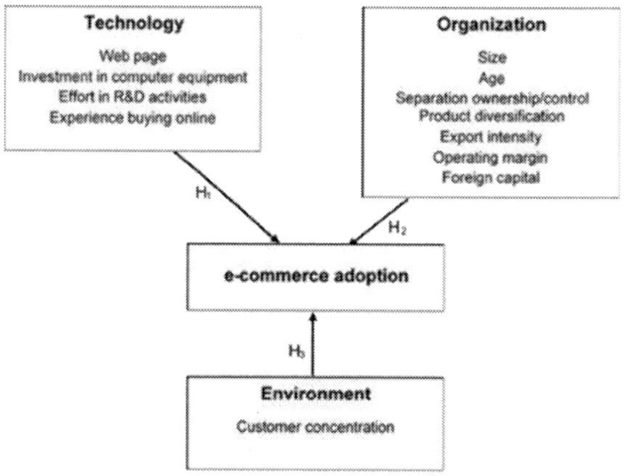

Figure 1. Proposed model for the B2C implementation by the Spanish manufacturing companies

C. *Sample characteristics*

The sample used comprises 14,029 firm-year observations obtained from 1,770 companies over the period 2001-2013. Tables II and III display some descriptive statistics for the dichotomous and continuous variables, respectively. For the former, frequencies and percentages are shown and for the latter, mean, standard deviation, minimum and maximum were computed.

TABLE I. VARIABLES IN THE ANALYSIS

Variable	Meaning
web-b2c	Business-to-consumer e-commerce. Dummy variable that equals 1 if the company makes B2C and 0 otherwise. This is the dependent variable of the model.
age	Number of years since the company was founded.
owner_control	Dummy variable indicating whether there is identity between ownership and control of the company. Equals one if the owners or their family are in management positions.
sales	Net sales of the company.
margin	Margin over operating income. Margin is defined as the sum of sales, changes in inventories and other current operating income less purchases, external services and personnel costs. Operating income is total sales plus the change in stocks and other current operating income.
con_conc	Consumers' concentration. Percent of the sales made to the three main customers over the total company sales.
diversif	Diversification of products. Equals 0 if the company manufactures only one product (at 3-digits classification level) and 1 otherwise.
for_cap	Percent of direct or indirect participation of foreign capital over the share capital of the company.
invcom	Investments in computer equipment. Percent of computer equipment purchases over investments in property, plant and equipment.
ownserver	Dummy variable indicating whether the Web page of the company is hosted on its own servers (1) or not (0).
intpurchases	Dummy variable indicating whether the company makes purchases through the Internet (1) or not (0).
rd_sales	Percent of R&D expenditure over total sales.
export_sales	Percent of exports over total sales.

TABLE II. FREQUENCIES OF THE DICHOTOMOUS VARIABLES

Variable	0	1	Total
web-b2c	13,258 (94.50%)	771 (5.50%)	14,029 (100%)
owner_control	8,224 (58.62%)	5,805 (41.38%)	14,029 (100%)
diversif	12,211 (87.04%)	1,818 (12.96%)	14,029 (100%)
ownserver	9,610 (68.50%)	4,419 (31.50%)	14,029 (100%)
intpurchases	10,567 (75.32%)	3,462 (24.68%)	14,029 (100%)

TABLE III. DESCRIPTIVE STATISTICS FOR THE CONTINUOUS VARIABLES

Variable	No. obs.	Mean	St. dev.	Min	Max
age	14,029	37.71787	21.639	10	179
sales	14,029	9.19×10^7	3.99×10^8	11.805	7.62×10^9
margin	14,029	7.027664	33.32573	-913.9	3.150.4
con_conc	14,029	44.21705	28.42819	1	100
for_cap	14,029	19.08675	38.22149	0	100
invcom	14,029	6.495524	17.40614	0	100
rd_sales	14,029	0.0085402	0.1076871	0	12.41273
export_sales	14,029	0.2163531	0.2776703	0	1

D. *Empirical Methods*

Random effects Logit panel-data estimations were used. The STATA 13.1 software package was used. The dependent variable is web-b2c, a dichotomous one, which equals 1 if the company makes sales to individual customers through the Internet and 0 otherwise. The independent variables are age, owner_control, sales, margin, con_conc, diversif, for_cap, invcom, ownserver, intpurchases, rd_sales, export_sales, and the dummy variables indicating the sector ascription (In order to avoid perfect collinearity we dropped the largest sector).

IV. RESULTS

Table IV contains the results of the panel logit regression estimation. We display the coefficients and their standard errors, as well as the z statistics and the corresponding p-values. We also include some additional statistics (Log likelihood and the corresponding test, and the ρ test on the significance of the panel variance).

The analysis of the ρ-statistic reveals that the panel-level variance is significant. Therefore, the use of a panel data approach is justified. Furthermore, the likelihood ratio test evidences the joint significance of the set of independent variables. With regard to the results for each one of the proposed indicators, the following results are obtained:

- Our data provide evidence to support H_{1a}, H_{1d}, H_{2a}, and H_{2b}. This implies that older and larger companies are more prone to the implementation of e-commerce. In addition, companies that have their own servers to host their websites and those who had previous experience in making purchases online are also more prone to the implementation of e-commerce.
- The results show that the higher the consumers' concentration, the less the propensity to implement e-commerce, and thus H_{3a} is confirmed. In addition, the companies that invest the most in computer equipment are less likely to implement e-commerce.

TABLE IV. RESULTS OF THE PANEL LOGIT REGRESSION

	Coef.	Std. Err.	z	P>z
age	*0.0123028*	*0.0057153*	*2.15*	*0.031*
owner_control	-0.2349963	0.1889312	-1.24	0.214
sales	5.51×10^{-10}	2.28×10^{-10}	*2.41*	*0.016*
margin	0.0001943	0.0030858	0.06	0.950
con_conc	*-0.0104101*	*0.003728*	*-2.79*	*0.005*
diversif	-0.0978172	0.2200009	-0.44	0.657
for_cap	0.0017419	0.0027105	0.64	0.520
invcom	*-0.0084241*	*0.0040836*	*-2.06*	*0.039*
ownserver	*1.514425*	*0.1661262*	*9.12*	*0.000*
intpurchases	*2.128654*	*0.1539428*	*13.83*	*0.000*
rd_sales	0.3449393	0.6762351	0.51	0.610
export_sales	-0.3080579	0.4131901	-0.75	0.456
Intercept	*-7.794592*	*0.5501702*	*-14.17*	*0.000*
Log likelihood	-1703.4359			
	Likelihood-ratio test:			
χ^2=434.46	p=0.000			
ρ	0.7557506	0.0207241		
	Likelihood-ratio test of ρ=0			
χ^2=1517.11	p=0.000			

This is the opposite of what we hypothesized (H_{1b}). As reasons for this, it is possible to point out that the implementation of this innovation requires, rather than an investment in physical equipment, the development of software projects, and companies that are forced to renew/expand their hardware may no longer have available resources to purchase/develop software products. This is because all these investments usually belong to the common chapter of technological investments within the company budget.

- For the other independent variables there seems to be no influence.

The results show the influence of factors belonging to the three contexts identified by the TOE framework in the e-commerce implementation.

V. Conclusions

Despite the positive effects of the adoption of e-commerce, a considerable number of Spanish companies have not yet implemented it. This situation differs from what happens in other European countries, where rates of use of e-commerce are much higher. This justifies the interest in knowing the characteristic factors of the companies that have adopted e-commerce.

The results obtained reveal the positive influence in the implementation of e-commerce of two relevant factors, which belong to the organizational context of the company: size and age. It seems clear that older and larger companies are perceived by consumers as more trustworthy and less risky, and this leads this kind of firms to implement e-commerce. Indeed, trust is considered a key factor for the success of e-commerce. This perception may move older and larger companies to implement e-commerce.

Two variables from the business technological context (whether the company makes purchases through the Internet, whether it has its own servers to host its website), are also shown as determining factors for the implementation of e-commerce.

Finally, as regards the environmental context, the evidence obtained supports that the dispersion of customers has an influence on the implementation of e-commerce.

It should be noted that the introduction of e-commerce is conditioned by the technological context, the organizational context and the environmental context of the company. This means that in order to increase the implementation rates, it is necessary to act on the three contexts at the same time. The results obtained show that the main measure to be taken is to reduce the uncertainty that any innovation process entails. Because of such uncertainty, the larger and the older (more experienced) companies are in better position for the implementation. However, the contagion effect that these companies exert on the others in any area makes more and more companies betting on it.

Finally, as future lines of research to develop the present paper, we propose to analyze the reasons why many companies still do not use e-commerce, even though the number decreases progressively over time. It should also be interesting to determine why some of the factors that were proven relevant in prior research conducted at the international level (ownership-control separation, margin, diversification, foreign capital, R&D intensity and exports) are not relevant for the Spanish case.

Acknowledgment

This paper was supported by the Spanish Minister of Economy and Competitiveness (Grant ECO2014-52519-R).

References

[1] National Commission of Markets and Competition, "E-Commerce Report" 2016. Available: https://telecos.cnmc.es/informes-comercio-electronico. [Last access: May 15, 2017].

[2] Statistics National Institute, "Survey on the use of Information and Communication Technologies (ICT) and electronic commerce in companies," 2016. Available: http://www.ine.es. [Last access: May 15, 2017].

[3] J. Gibbs, K. Kraemer, and J. Dedrick, "Environment and policy factors shaping global e-commerce diffusion: A crosscountry comparison," The Information Society, vol. 19, nº 1, pp. 5-18, 2003.

[4] K. Tan, S.-C. Chong, and B. Lin, "Intention to use Internet marketing: A comparative study between Malaysians and South Koreans," Kybernetes, vol. 42, nº 6, pp. 889-905, 2013.

[5] C. Yoon, "The effects of national culture values on consumer acceptance of e-commerce: Online shoppers in China," Information and Management, vol. 46, nº 5, pp. 294-301, 2009.

[6] L. Tornatzky and M. Fleischer, The processes of technological innovation, Lexington, MA: Lexington Books, 1990.

[7] Y. Wang and P. Ahmed, "The moderating effect of the business strategic orientation on eCommerce adoption: Evidence from UK family run SMEs," Journal of Strategic Information System, vol. 18, pp. 16-30, 2008.

[8] I. Arpaci, Y. Yardimci, S. Ozkan, and O. Turetken, "Organizational adoption of information technologies: A literature review," International Journal of eBusiness and eGovernment Studies, vol. 2, pp. 37-50, 2012.

[9] W. Ismail and A. Ali, "Conceptual model for examining the factors that influence the likelihood of computerised accounting information system (CAIS) adoption among Malaysian SMES," International Journal of Information Technology and Business Management, vol. 15, nº 1, p. 122–151, 2013.

[10] K. Ven and J. Verelst, "An empirical investigation into the assimilation of opensource server software," Communications of the Association for Information Systems, vol. 9, p. 117–140, 2011.

[11] K. Zhu, K. Kraemer, and S. Xu, "E-business adoption by European firms: a cross-country assessment of the facilitators and inhibitors," European Journal of Information Systems, vol. 12, nº 4, pp. 251-268, 2003.

[12] H. Lin and S. Lin, "Determinants of e-business diffusion: A test of the technology diffusion perspective," Technovation, vol. 28, nº 3, pp. 135-145, 2008.

[13] B. Ramdani and P. Kawaiek, "SME Adoption of Enterprise Systems in the Northwest of England: An Environmental, Technological and Organizational Perspective," de IFIP WG 8.6 - Organizational Dynamics of Technology-Based Innovation: Diversifying the Research Agenda, Springer, 2007, pp. 409-429.

[14] T. Teo, M. Tan, and W. Buk, "A contingency model of Internet adoption in Singapore," International Journal of Electronic Commerce, vol. 2, nº 2, pp. 95-118, 1997.

[15] I. Ahmad and A. Agrawal, "An Empirical Study of Problems in Implementation of Electronic Commerce in Kingdom of Saudi Arabia," International Journal of Business and Management, vol. 7, n° 15, pp. 70-80, 2012.

[16] M. Cao, Q. Zhang, and J. Seydel, "B2C e-commerce web site quality: an empirical examination," Industrial Management & Data Systems, vol. 105, n° 5, pp. 645-661, 2005.

[17] M. To and E. Ngai, "Predicting the organisational adoption of B2C e-commerce: an empirical," Industrial Management & Data Systems, vol. 106, n° 8, pp. 1133-1147, 2006.

[18] Z. Acs, P. Braunerhjelm, D. Audretsch, and B. Carlsson, "The knowledge spillover theory of enterpreneurship," Small Business Economics, vol. 32, n° 1, pp. 15-30, 2009.

[19] S. Bowde et al."Adoption and implementation of e-business in New Zealand: preliminary results," in Proceedings of the 9th Annual Conference of the New Zealand Strategic Management Society, 2000.

[20] R. Sultana, J.-L. Lopez, and L. Rusu, "Barriers to e-Commerce Implementation in Small Enterprises in Sweden," de CENTERIS 2011, Part I, CCIS 219, Springer-Verlag Berlin Heidelberg, 2011, pp. 178-189.

[21] H. Hwang, C. Ku, D. Yen, and C. Cheng, "Critical factors influencing the adoption of data warehouse technology: a study of the banking industry in Taiwan," Decision Support Systems, vol. 1, pp. 1-21, 2004.

[22] W. Cohen and R. Levin, "Empirical studies of innovation and market structure," in Handbook of Industrial Organization, Vol. II, North Holland, Amsterdam: Elsevier, 1989, p. 1059–1107.

[23] P. Pool, J. Parnell, J. Spillan, S. Carraher, and D. Lester, "Are SMEs meeting the challenge of integrating e-commerce into their businesses? A review of the development, challenges and opportunities," International Journal of Information Technology and Management, vol. 5, n° 2-3, pp. 97-113, 2006.

[24] J. Weltevreden and R. Boschma, "Internet strategies and performance of Dutch retailers," Journal of Retailing and Consumer Services, vol. 15, n° 3, pp. 163-178, 2008.

[25] T. Chuang, K. Nakatani, J. Chen, and I. Huang, "Examining the impact of organisational and owner's characteristics on the extent of e-commerce adoption in SMEs," International Journal of Business and Systems Research, vol. 1, n° 1, pp. 61-80, 2007.

[26] B. Jean, K. Han, and M. Lee, "Determining factors for the adoption of e-business: the case of SMEs in Korea," Applied Economics, vol. 38, n° 16, pp. 1905-1916, 2006.

[27] B. Levitt and J. March, "Organizational learning," Annual Review of Sociology, vol. 14, pp. 319-340, 1988.

[28] A. Coad, A. Segarra, and M. Teruel, "Innovation and firm growth: Does firm age play a role?," Research Policy, vol. 45, pp. 387-400, 2016.

[29] M. Tripsas and G. Gavetti, "Capabilities, cognition, and inertia: evidence from digital imaging," Strategic Management Journal, vol. 21, n° 10-11, pp. 1147-1161, 2000.

[30] T. Oliveira and M. Martins, "Understanding e-business adoption across industries in European countries," Industrial Management & Data Systems, vol. 110, n° 9, pp. 1337-1354, 2010.

[31] N. Kumar and M. Saqib, "Firm size, opportunities for adaptation and in-house R & D activity in developing countries: the case of Indian manufacturing," Research Policy, vol. 25, n° 5, pp. 713-722, 1996.

[32] G. Premkumar and M. Roberts, "Adoption of new information technologies in rural small business," OMEGA, International Journal of Management Science, vol. 27, n° 4, p. 467–484, 1999.

[33] M. Berry and J. Brock, "Market space and the Internationalization Process of the Small Firm," Journal of International Entrepreneurship, vol. 2, n° 3, pp. 187-216, 2004.

[34] F. Damanpour and S. Gopalakrishnan, "The Dynamics of the Adoption of Product and Process Innovations in Organizations," Journal of Management Studies, vol. 38, n° 1, pp. 45-65, 2001.

[35] A. Gourlay and E. Pentecost, "The Determinants of Technology Diffusion: Evidence from the UK Financial Sector" The Manchester School, vol. 70, n° 2, pp. 185-203, 2002.

[36] E. Abrahamson and L. Rosenkopf, "Social Network Effects on the Extent of Innovation Diffusion: A Computer Simulation" Organization Science, vol. 8, n° 3, pp. 289-309, 1997.

[37] S. Al-Somali, R. Gholami, and B. Clegg, "Determinants of B2B E-Commerce Adoption in Saudi Arabian Firms," International Journal of Digital Society, vol. 2, n° 2, pp. 406-414, 2011.

[38] K. Soliman and B. Janz, "An exploratory study to identify the critical factors affecting the decision to establish Internet-based interorganizational information systems," Information and Management, vol. 41, n° 6, p. 697–706, 2004.

[39] P. DiMaggio and W. Powell, "The Iron Cage Revisited: Institutional Isomorphism and Collective Rationality in Organizational Fields," American Sociological Review, vol. 48, n° 2, pp. 147-160, 1983.

[40] H. Hollenstein, "The decision to adopt information and communication technologies (ICT): firm-level evidence for Switzerland," in The Economic Impact of ICT. Measurement, Evidence and Implications, Paris, OECD, 2004, pp. 37-60.

[41] L. Piris, G. Fitzgerald, and A. Serrano, "Strategic motivators and expected benefits from e-commerce in traditional organizations," International Journal of Information Management, vol. 24, pp. 489-506, 2004.

Proposal of Continuous Audit Model

Data Integration Framework

Mauricio Mello Codesso
Graduate Program of Accounting
Federal University of Santa Catarina - UFSC
Florianopolis, Brazil
mmcodesso@gmail.com

Rogerio Joao Lunkes
Graduate Program of Accounting
Federal University of Santa Catarina - UFSC
Florianopolis, Brazil
rogerio.lunkes@ufsc.br

Paulo Caetano da Silva
Graduate Program of Information Systems
University of Salvador – UNIFACS
paulo.caetano@pro.unifacs.br

Abstract—**The approximation of business areas with the use of new technologies, real-time savings, transactions with several countries and on several continents with different law guarantees are necessary. These warranties can be acquired through Continuous Audit (CA). Some research contributions may be listed as: provide a standardization of data and nomenclatures for the data used by Continuous Audit procedures; re-use of previously developed detection and analysis algorithms; reduction of the development and implementation costs of the processes of continuous audit in organizations due to the standardization of data and the reutilization of algorithm; encouragement for the creation of a repository of public access algorithms. The paper also aims to contribute to the literature with the deepening of ways to access, structure and collect critical and / or necessary data for CA. With the deepening of Audit Data Standard and eXtensible Business Reporting Language (XBRL), as well as creating a basis for future research with the integration of extraction, analysis and exception detection algorithms that are used by CA.**

Keywords-Continuous Audit; XBRL; Audit; Audit Framework

I. INTRODUCTION

Real-time economics and globalization have caused an increase in the amount of data that is captured and stored. This change is also facilitated by lower costs of storage, e-commerce, and increased use of information technology in business, such as Enterprise Resource Planning (ERP) systems, which generate huge amounts of transactional data for users. Various business systems have been developed to support decision making, planning and control, as well as monitoring organizational performance [1][2]. However, this phenomenon of high data volume requires a different approach to audit.

After conducting a global fraud research, the Association of Certified Fraud Examiners found that fraud costs organizations 5% of their annual income. The average time to detect and report frauds was 18 months. Confidence has been in traditional external audits as the primary fraud detection technique, however, these have only accounted for 3% of frauds. On the other hand, the implementation of controls to detect frauds has been proven effectiveness in reducing costs and extent of fraud [3].

Companies are increasingly dependent on computerized systems, such as ERPs, to handle their business processes. This process of business computerization, coupled with real-time economics, encourages and requires companies to generate data in a timely manner. To extract useful information, and finally knowledge that can support decision making [4], it is essential to ensure the quality and reliability of this data [5].

Advances in technology enable real-time or near-real-time monitoring; however, audit services have evolved at a much slower pace. Most of these services are still performed manually, an approach that is time-consuming and costly [6]. This comes in contrast to the technology currently available, which can offer ongoing credibility support.

Various aspects of the audit need to be reviewed. While traditional audit takes a sample-based approach, mainly due to time constraints and budgets, continuous audit examines the entire population of record. Companies can benefit from the use of automation and technology to improve the efficiency and effectiveness of auditing through the implementation of continuous auditing systems. Companies can lower the cost of work associated with audits by taking advantage of computerized technology and systems. In addition, this can increase the efficiency of their production [7][8].

Continuous Audit is an audit process that produces audit results simultaneously or in a short time after a relevant event occurs [9]. The continuous auditing implementation is only feasible as a fully automated process and with immediate access to relevant events and their results. To meet these requirements, systems must be permanently connected, for both auditors and auditees.

Continuous auditing begins to gain more space as organizations gain more automation in their business processes and, therefore, the requirements for monitoring business risk [10]. However, the development of continuous auditing has enormous technological and organizational challenges. The wide variety of software used in companies makes it difficult for auditors to develop integrated auditing systems. Many pieces of such software were designed as stand-alone systems, with little or no network communication capability. However, the current stage of ERP development demonstrates a greater tendency for standardization and better integration with other subsystems [11].

Traditional audits and the use of small sampling techniques are progressively less effective when dealing with large volumes of data. Unlike traditional auditing, continuous auditing does not work with samples, it analyzes the entire transaction population, which allows the change from manual detection to the development of prevention capabilities [12]. O'Reilly [13] points out the benefits generated using CA methodologies:

- Make the audit process faster, cheaper, more efficient and more effective;
- Reduce the time needed for audit cycles, providing better response times for risk control and reliability of operations;
- Increase the coverage of audit work without increasing the amount of resources needed;
- Enable the conduction of audits daily, monthly or in the interval of time that is deemed appropriate;
- Automate periodic audit testing, improving audit execution time;
- Test 100% of the data population in the audit work and not just a sample;
- Improve the quality of the audit and its speed.

CA allows corrective action to be taken sooner than traditional approaches. The focus of the audit will shift from manual detection to technology-based prevention [14]. The CA allows the auditor to analyze the data more frequently by performing control and risk assessment in a real-time environment. It allows the opportunity to go beyond traditional auditing approaches, such as sampling and analyzing at a specific point in time, providing automatic and timely detection of failures in controls and exception situations, directing efforts to find the facts and remedies needed [12].

Real-time monitoring techniques can reduce errors and fraud, increase operational efficiency and profits [12]. Sarbanes & Oxley (SOX) defines rules and conditions for auditing and controlling operational risks, which has created complex demands for companies. The legal requirement of financial statements to be published in real time led to the need for transactions to also be audited in real time [14].

The required control for compliance with legislation has forced companies to look for ways to meet this requirement at acceptable costs. The CA has been gaining strength due to the possibility of automating risk control through the early perception of possible problems, by using internal control to act in a preventive and no longer detective way [12].

Continuous auditing and monitoring can improve the efficiency of auditing work through automation and adoption of an audit-by-exception approach. In this approach, the total population is analyzed and only exceptions are investigated. This is a type of audit that can be done more often, in which exceptions are identified, and alarms are sent to those responsible to correct these errors. If they fail to correct the errors in a timely manner, the internal audit department may be notified to act [15].

In the literature, there are numerous studies that use statistical tests and techniques to identify exceptions [16] [17]. The proposed methodologies are efficient in helping auditors to identify anomalies and exceptions [18] [19]. However, these studies do not integrate with each other, and do not address the issue of data availability and extraction ways.

Flowerday et al. [14] describe problems affecting continuous auditing solutions is the variety of data formats and records, including legacy systems that are crucial to creating continuous audit system. For this, it is necessary that there is an evaluation and standardization of this data so that there are no processing errors.

The standardization of data format is the most complex and challenging aspect for building CA capabilities, which may entail high costs and complexity due to the need to collect information from different systems [20].

In light of the exposed issues and the difficulties pointed out by previous studies, the following problem question arises: How to standardize the data of the various systems so that it is possible to implement continuous audit?

A. *Research Objetives*

The general objective of the paper is to propose the development of a framework for integration of different systems for continuous auditing.

B. *Specific Objetives*

- Identify the structure of XBRL and Audit Data Standard templates;
- Define methodology and definition of classes and attributes;
- Identify flowchart of processes and data;
- Test the model and framework

II. BACKGROUND

Continuous Audit studies present as difficulties the availability and high cost of data access for the implementation of monitoring routines. As a consequence, what is lacking in the academic and professional literature is a deeper analysis of how to collect, structure, and elaborate sampling of critical data for Audit analysis. This omission of methods and standards can undermine the work of the auditor by multiplying his sample bases beyond what is necessary, which will lead to auditing in a larger number of substantive tests as well as too many analytical procedures [21]. The ability to access and retrieve information from a variety of sources, including legacy systems, is a crucial point in creating a CA system. This makes it important to standardize data. However, this can be a complex and costly process [14].

The high investments required for CA implementation are pointed out in [14] as a difficulty to be overcome for adoption. Similarly, the financial scandals that occurred in large organizations over the last decade, due to the execution of internal frauds, have amplified the performance of the audit, which needs to carry out analyzes in an instantaneous way and in opportune moments. In addition, the rigidity of regulatory requirements, such as the Sarbanes & Oxley (SOX) Act and Corporate Governance principles that offer a high level of transparency and an organized and well-managed internal control environment, have increased the importance of Auditing, be it internal or external [21].

The need for instant and steady security about the efficiency of risk management and the internal control environment is critical. Organizations are exposed to significant errors, fraud and inefficiencies that can lead to financial losses and increased risk exposure [22].

A. Research Contributions

The paper aims to contribute empirically, with the development of a framework for the application of CA in organizations. This will help companies in their projects of Continuous Audit.

The approximation of the business areas with the use of new technologies, real-time savings, transactions with several countries and in several continents with different law guarantees. are necessary. These warranties can be acquired through AC. Some research contributions may be listed as:

- Provide a standardization of data and nomenclatures for the data used by Continuous Audit procedures;
- Re-use of previously developed detection and analysis algorithms;
- Reduction of the development and implementation costs of the processes of continuous audit in the organizations due to the standardization of data and the reutilization of algorithm;
- Encourage the creation of a repository of public access algorithms.

The paper also aims to contribute to the literature with the deepening of ways to access, structure and collect critical and / or necessary data for CA. With the deepening of Audit Data Standard and XBRL, as well as creating a basis for future research with the integration of extraction, analysis and exception detection algorithms that are used by CA.

References

[1] Bernhard, A. How Big Data brings BI, predictive analytics together, 2012. Disponível em http://www.cio.com/article/716726/ How_Big_Data_Brings_BI_Predictive_Analytics_Together.

[2] Vijayan, J. (2012). Finding the business value in big data is a big problem. Disponível em http://www.computerworld.com/s/article/ 9231224/ Finding_the_business_value_in_big_data_is_a_big_proble m

[3] Ratley, J. Report to the Nations: On occupational fraud and abuse. 2012. Disponível em http://www.acfe.com/uploadedFiles/ACFE_ Website/Content/rttn/2012-report-to-nations.pdf.

[4] Elliott, R., Kielich, J. Expert systems for accountants. Journal of Accountancy,1985.

[5] Vasarhelyi, M., Chan, D., Krahel, J. (2012). Consequences of XBRL standardization on financial statement data. Journal of Information Systems. v. 26, n. 1, 2012, p. 155-167.

[6] Vasarhelyi, M., Alles, M., Williams, K. Continuous assurance for the now economy. Sydney, Australia: Institute of Chartered Accountants in Australia, 2010

[7] Elliott, R. Assurance services and the audit heritage. CPA Journal, 68(6),1998, p. 40.

[8] Menon, K., Williams, D. Long-term trends in audit fees. Auditing: A Journal of Practice & Theory, 2001.

[9] Vasarhelyi, M., Romero, S., Kuenkaikaew, S., Littley, J. Adopting Continuous Audit/ Continuous Monitoring in Internal Audit. ISACA Journal vol. 3, 2012, P. 31

[10] Vasarhelyi, M.; Alles, M; Kogan, A. Principles of analytic monitoring for continuous assurance. Journal of Emerging Technologies in Accounting, v.1, p.1-21, 2004

[11] Kogan, A., Sudit, E., Vasarhelyi, M. Continuous online auditing: a program of research. Journal of Information Systems, 13(2), 1999, p. 87–103.

[12] Li, Y. et al. Achieving Sarbanes-oxley compliance with XBRL-based ERP and Continuous Auditing. Issues in Information Systems, v. VIII n. 2, 2007, p. 430-436

[13] O'Reilly, A. Continuous auditing: wave of the future?. Corporate Board, set./oct. 2006.

[14] Flowerday, S.; Blundell, A.; Von Solms, R. Continuous auditing technologies and models: A discussion. Computer & Security. n. 25, 2006, p. 325-331.

[15] Alles, M., Kogan, A., Vasarhelyi, M. Putting continuous auditing theory into practice: Lessons from two pilot implementations. Journal of Information Systems, 22(2), 2008, p. 195–214.

[16] Dull, R., Tegarden, D., Schleifer, L. Actve: a proposal for an automated continuous transaction verification environment. Journal of Emerging Technologies, 3(1), 2006, p. 81–96.

[17] Groomer, S., MURTHY, U. Continuous auditing of database applications: An embedded audit module approach. Journal of Information Systems, 3(2),1989, p. 53–69.

[18] Alles, M., Brennan, G., Kogan, A., Vasarhelyi, M. Continuous monitoring of business process controls: A pilot implementation of a continuous auditing system at Siemens. International Journal of Accounting A42Information Systems, 7(2), 2006, p. 137–161.

[19] Debreceny, R., Gray, G., Tham, W., Goh, K., Tang, P. The Development of Embedded Audit Modules to Support Continuous Monitoring, Electronic Commerce Environment, 185, 2003, p. 169–185.

[20] Rezaee, Z. et al. Continuous auditing: Building Automated Auditing Capability. Auditing. Journal of Practice & Theory. v. 21 n. 1, 2002, p.147-163.

[21] Silva, W. Auditoria contínua de dados como instrumento de automação do controle empresarial. 2012. Tese (Doutorado em Sistemas Digitais) - Escola Politécnica, Universidade de São Paulo, São Paulo, 2012.

[22] Bumgarner, N., Vasarhelyi, M. Continuous Auditing - A New View, Audit Analytics and Continuous Audit: Looking Toward The Future, AICPA, New York, 2015.

FVA: Financial Virtual Assistant

Adalberto Alves Abraão, Paulo Caetano da Silva
UNIFACS - Universidade Salvador
Salvador, Brazil
e-mail: adalbertoabraao@gmail.com, paulo.caetano@pro.unifacs.br

Abstract— **Getting information about the current and past financial situation of a company is important before investing in this company. Extracting this information from an information system that uses taxonomy recognized by the financial markets using natural language, is a facility for the investor who has no knowledge and no expertise in computer science. The virtual assistance software are alternatives to help people in an area of knowledge. However, it is observed that there is no information system that interacts with the user through natural language to answer questions about financial information of companies, based on data available in electronic financial disclosures. This paper presents a computational system of virtual assistance, named Financial Virtual Assistant (FVA), which recognizes user questions relating to financial situation of companies, through text, or voice, in natural language. This system provides answers based on available information in electronic financial statements represented in eXtensible Business Reporting Language (XBRL) technology. The system's implementation is based on a proposed architecture for specific purpose virtual assistants that uses a Natural Language Processor (NLP) and the domain information services. Details of this architecture, the system's implementation and the used natural language processing configuration are presented. During testing, the Assistant correctly answered all financial questions about certain companies in a compatible average period with available generic virtual assistants in the market. Besides that, the Assistant could to talk to the user, simulating a conversation between people.**

Keywords-Financial Virtual Assistant; FVA; Virtual Assistants Architecture; Specific Purpose Assistant; XBRL US-GAAP.

I. INTRODUCTION

Usually, financial consulting services provided by an assistant or a financial advisor are very expensive. For a small investor with limited resources to hire a financial professional, a computer system that provides service virtually through answers to questions using natural language can be an alternative to this kind of financial advice. However, the virtual assistant software, usually embedded in smartphones, e.g., Siri [1], Cortana [2] and Google Now [3], provides inaccurate responses to the questions about companies' financial information. Normally, these answers correspond to a list of links to financial sites.

Actually, the available financial information to investors on the market are disclosure by the technology XBRL [4] that is derived from XML and it was created to facilitate the exchange data and financial information. Most of the world's major stock exchanges operate with this technology, e.g., US-SEC (U.S. Securities and Exchange Commission), the European market, Tokyo. Therefore, extracting information represented by XBRL technology is an important source to support the financial questions for decision-making on investments.

After conducting a literature review, we did not find any academic paper, or market solution, related to the financial virtual assistants of question and answers type. However, proposed frameworks and architectures for building virtual assistants have been found. To fill this gap, this paper presents the FVA, based on XBRL technology, that answers financial questions using natural language, in different languages, e.g., English and Portuguese. Therefore, the aim of this paper is to present the architecture and implementation of a computer system of virtual assistance question/answer type that interacts with the costumer using natural language to answer questions about financial state of companies that provide their financial statements on the market. This system supports a conversation with the user too. This paper is organized as follows: Section II discusses some related works; in Section III, the architecture of the FVA is proposed; the presentation of FVA implementation is presented in Section IV; in Section V, the results of the FVA tests are evaluated and in Section VI the conclusion is presented.

II. RELATED WORKS

The architecture for creating specific purpose assistants in [5] allows the expansion of knowledge and behavior of an assistant by adding new services. This architecture predicts the interaction with the user through natural language and supports the dialog management. However, it was designed for agents' technology in [6], which is in disuse. One of the agents' disadvantages is the need for a specific environment for the agents, and many of these environments were discontinued.

The architecture reference for a specific purpose assistants in [7] was designed to build assistants that help the user to explore a specific Web site. So, the created assistants based on this architecture, do not provide precise and complete answers. The architecture in [8], which allows the creation of assistants that may have their expanded knowledge by third-party services, does not provide resources for user interactions in natural language, in addition to the dialogue management being restricted by user interface applications.

The architecture of the Virtual Assistant [9] allows users to enlarge your knowledge by adding new plugins. This feature enables the creation and addition of a financial knowledge module. This architecture is implemented by Syn Engine platform [10]. Their drawbacks are it supports only one language (English), and it is available only for two software environments that limits the number of users. For the Assistant.ai assistant [11], only part of its architecture is available. This part is the area responsible for conversation maintenance with the user and is based on a NLP. One of the disadvantages of using this architecture is that it is not complete, i.e., some sections are not available, e.g., the area responsible for the selection and extraction of information domain, the area responsible for the construction of the answers to the user. Architectures of market assistants, e.g., Siri, Google Now and Cortana, are not available.

After the literature review, it is concluded that these architectures and frameworks do not support the creation of a FVA based on XBRL technology that answers financial questions using natural language, in different languages, simulating a conversation between people.

III. FVA ARHITECTURE

The proposed architecture for the FVA is designed to create assistants, question/answer type, to distributed and service-oriented environment. This architecture is an extension of the architecture we presented in [12]. One of the reasons for this architecture design be service-oriented is to facilitate the expansion of behaviors and knowledge of the assistant, through adding new services. This architecture consists of four layers categorized by their functions: Presentation, Orchestration, Understanding / Knowledge and Data, as illustrated in Figure 1.

The Presentation layer is the user interface layer. It is responsible for interaction with the user and forwarding the user requests to the Orchestration layer and presenting the replies that were sent by the Orchestration, to the user in the proper format, i.e., text or voice. The assistant usability depends directly on the Presentation layer. The Orchestration layer is the layer that coordinates the Assistant, manages the knowledge assistant and manages the dialog with the user. It is responsible for making the decision of what should be done in response to the stimuli provided by the Presentation and Understanding / Knowledge layers, also it is responsible for the treatment of any services and / or components failure. In addition to triggering the services of Understanding / Knowledge Layer and forwarding the responses to the Presentation Layer, it also verifies whether the information passed by the user is complete for obtaining an answer or some additional information is still needed. The Assistant robustness depends directly on this layer. The Understanding / Knowledge Layer is the assistant cognitive center. It interprets the user information, it provides the recognized information to decision-making process and it provides the specialized information services in the financial field to Orchestration Layer.

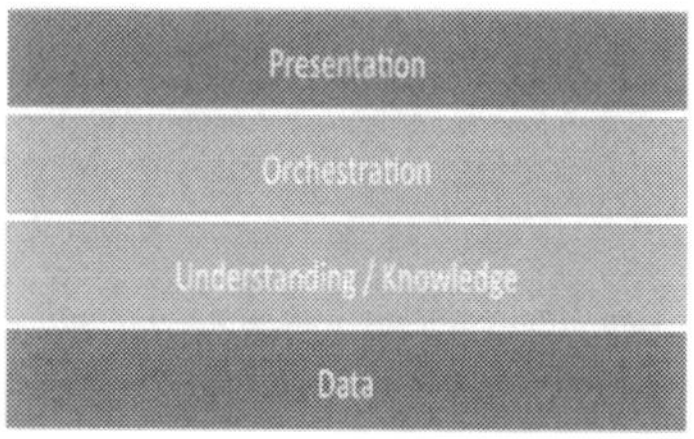

Figure 1. Architecture in layers of the FVA

The Understanding / Knowledge Layer corresponds to the knowledge domain of the Assistant. The greater the knowledge represented by this Layer, the more intelligent and knowledgeable in the financial field is the assistant. The Data layer is responsible for providing the data to the Understanding / Knowledge layer. The reliability of assistant answers is proportional directly for the reliability of the data provided by this layer. The amount of information provided by the assistant is directly influenced by the data amount that this layer has access to.

Although the architecture is designed for the financial sector, it can be used for another domain. The organization of its components is such that it allows the incorporation of multidisciplinary, multilingual and user interaction features. Figure 2 shows the details of each layer that are discussed in the next section.

A. Details of architecture components

The Speech To Text (STT), which is a speech to text converter, and The Text To Speech (TTS), which is a text to speech converter, allow interaction by voice between the Assistant and the user. These components access the dictionaries that are databases responsible for supporting the conversions speech to text, and vice versa, for different languages. The User Interface Manager (UIM) is responsible for user interaction, it collects user questions and forwards to the Orchestration layer and waits for the response to present to the user. It also, with the help of STT and TTS, interacts with the user using voice. The presentation of the answer to the user is also the responsibility of the UIM.

The Coordinator is responsible for controlling the life cycle of each question session initiated by the user and for managing the assistant's information flow. The Coordinator is responsible for collecting user requests sent by UIM, and forwarding the question text to the NLP, and getting the NLP answer that is the identification of the user's intention and the parameters that have been recognized in the user question. In addition, the Coordinator is responsible for interacting with Dialog and Knowledge Manager (DKM) for getting the answer to the user, and forwarding it to the UIM, besides its responsibility to treat the failures of the layers with which it interacts. The DKM is the manager of the dialogue with the user and knowledge manager of the Assistant. The DKM uses the context information for supportting the maintenance of the dialogue with the user, simulating a conversation between people. The knowledge management that is its other responsability, is the configuration and maintenance of services belonging to the financial domain in Understanding / Knowledge Layer (UK). The NLP has the responsibility to

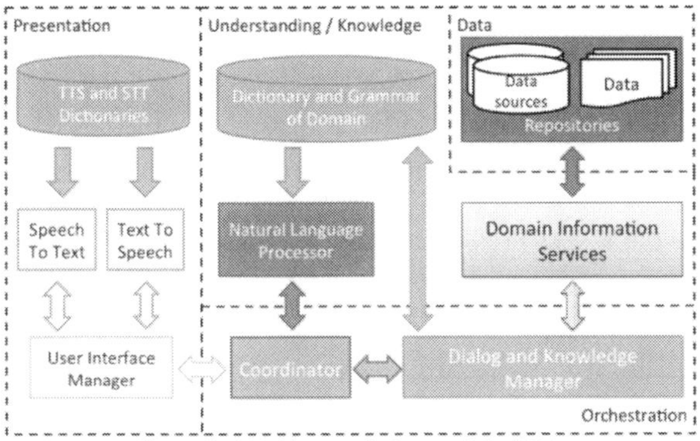

Figure 2. Architecture in layers of the FVA

recognize the user question, made in natural language, and extract parameterized information that is processable for a computer system. For manipulating the knowledge, the NLP needs the dictionary and grammar of the domain, i.e., after receiving a sentence, it queries the domain's dictionary and grammar in order to understand the sentence. Assistants based on this architecture will recognize requests that contain terms of this dictionary that correspond to the standard questions that were previously defined in the grammar. For the FVA, the dictionary and grammar domain of the NLP is financial. However, other domains, with related and proper dictionary and grammar, may be incorporated. The Domain Information Services are responsible for handling the available data in the Data layer and provide domain information requested by the Orchestration layer. These services represent the knowledge domain of the assistant, i.e., the greater scope of the domain information services available, the greater is the representation of knowledge in the assistant. For the FVA, they are called the Financial Information Services. Its ability to answer complex questions, e.g., financial analyzes and comparisons, depends on the availability of these services. The services of Data Layer correspond to repositories that provide data, e.g., a relational database, a data service delivery on the Web. For the FVA, the use of XBRL Repositories for providing financial data, was planned. This repositories can be composed of XBRL documents in XBRL databases or financial information services based on XBRL data. The taxonomy used by XBRL repository is also an item that interferes with the responses relevance of the FVA in relation to the financial area, because this taxonomy has to have representation in the financial domain.

One of the main advantages of the presented architecture is the prediction of the use of a natural language processing service, allowing substitution of NLP service for another, or even to use more than one service of this kind. This feature facilitates the implementation of multi-language virtual assistants of specific purpose, or assistants that recognize the vocabulary of different domains. This feature also facilitates the use of different natural language processing services that are available in the market or in the academic community. The architecture also provides for the dynamic update of the terms and grammar of domain. The isolation of the layers responsible for the knowledge domain and cognition of the assistant, and the voice converter services in the presentation layer, are characterized as another advantage, because it allows the maintenance of knowledge domain in a single layer and also the creation of virtual assistants that interact with the users exclusively through voice, without requiring complex coding in the user interface.

One of the limitations of this architecture is that it does not support the implementation of any specific purpose assistants, i.e., it is designed to build virtual assistants of question/answer type. The autonomous virtual assistants that autonomously perform a task, or a sequence of tasks, according to the context, are not supported by this architecture.

IV. Implementation Of The FVA

The implementation of the layers occurred almost entirely in a server environment, except for the Presentation layer that had one of its components implemented in the customer environment. The UIM was the only implemented component of the Presentation layer, because it is specific for the FVA. An Android application that supports voice recognition using TTS and STT services (provided by the Google), was coded, and a page javascript / html was coded too. The Orchestration Layer components were implemented with Java technology to run on a Web server that allows the Web client requests to be treated by the Assistant. Several Java classes were implemented, whose main classes for this layer are shown in class diagram in Figure 3.

The Coordinator class that was implemented as a Java Servlet, has the function of controlling the flow of information and trigger the basic components and services of

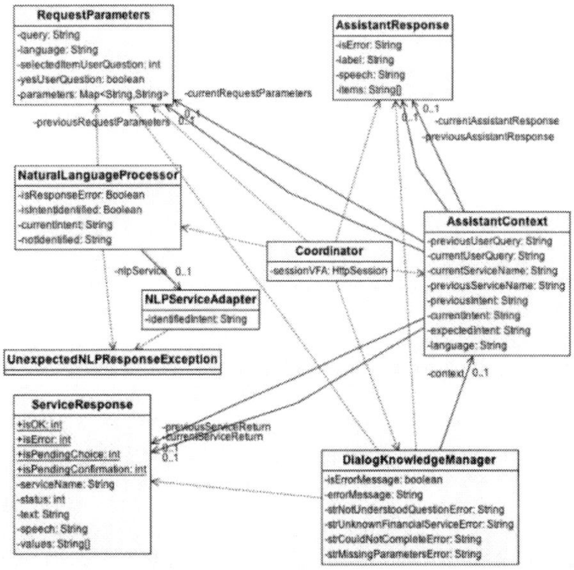

Figure 3. Class Diagram of implementation of The Orchestration Layer

the Assistant. The Coordinator class does not handle any information related to the financial domain; the AssistantContext class corresponds to the context of the information about the dialogue session with the user; the RequestParameters class stores all the information related to the user's query parameters; the NaturalLanguageProcessor and NLPServiceAdapter classes are the representatives of the NLP. To replace the NLP by another, just change the NLPServiceAdapter class; the AssistantResponse class corresponds to the Assistant answer for the user's question; the DialogKnowledgeManager class represents the Dialog and Knowledge Manager component, whose responsibility is to manage the knowledge of the Assistant and the dialogue between the Assistant and the user; the ServiceResponse class corresponds to the response of the service information to query submitted.

The Understanding / Knownledge Layer was implemented through Web Services. For the NLP, a conversational platform was used. This platform, named Api.ai [13], provides an NLP service for recognizing user expressions in different languages, e.g., English, Spanish and Portuguese. This platform enables the creation of services or components that can be configured to recognize expressions made in natural language related to different knowledge domains. The Financial Information Services have been implemented specifically for the FVA. Two pairs of dictionary of terms / grammar, one for the Portuguese language and other for English language, were built to represent the financial domain. The dictionary of terms is a database where the synonyms of domain concepts, names, keywords and the definition of a corresponding default value are registered. Many groupings of terms, whose denomination is entity, have been created. These entities have been divided into financial and generic types. They are used in grammar rules to indicate, for the NLP, which position in the user's expression the terms are expected. The configuration of the grammar rules was according to grammars' rules setting of the Api.ai NLP, e.g., for English version grammar, the question "What are the current liabilities of Petrobras in 2015" is captured by NLP according to the following rule:

[@greeting] [@CommandExpressions] @USGAAP_BalanceSheet:financialConcept [of] @Company:companyData [company] [in,on] @YearPeriod:yearPeriod [at, in, on fiscal year, in fiscal year, of fiscal year, of year, year] @sys.number:year

In this example, the subsequent expressions to @ symbol correspond to entities of dictionary of terms.

The words or phrases between brackets, inform that the occurrence of them is optional. To identify the user's intention, the grouping of grammatical rules has been used. The performed configuration identifies at least 14 intentions, e.g., "What is the Financial Concept of Company"; "What is the Variation of Financial Ratio of Company in the last period of time"; "Change the company". To represent the organization of the Financial Information Services, a Web Service compatible with the SOAP protocol was implemented. This Web Service has a method that requires two input parameters: a string that corresponds to the name of the service and the second string that corresponds to an instance of the RequestParameters class encapsulated in JSON format [14]. The answer of this Web Service corresponds to an instance of ServiceResponse class that is encapsulated in JSON format. The main function of this Web Service is to trigger the corresponding financial information service. One of the services, triggered by this Web Service, was implemented by CompanyRatioInformationService class, which provides text responses in natural language contains the value of index, or concept, of a financial company in a specified period.

The CompanyRatioInformationService class constructs messages with the answer of the Assistant, in Portuguese or English, and for that, it consumes data from another Web Service that represents the Data layer and it was implemented by XbrlUsgaapWebService class. This Web Service provides data from the US-SEC [15] through the SOAP protocol, and supports the following input parameters: USGAAPElementName that corresponds to the compatible XBRL element name with the US GAAP taxonomy [16]; cik, which is the CIK code of the company; year that corresponds to the year of the financial period; period, which corresponds to the part of year of the financial period. The result is a text provided in XML with structured financial data. The data source of the XbrlUsgaapWebService is the service of XBRL-US that provides the extracted data of the financial statements of companies provided by US-SEC. These statements are in XBRL format, in accordance with US-GAAP taxonomy. For the use of other XBRL taxonomy, e.g., IFRS, GRI, another configuration of this layer is necessary.

One of the advantages of the uncoupling, through the implementation of services, is the ease of maintenance of each component or service and the independence of the technology on which the service was implemented. One of the disadvantages of the implementation by services is the risk of delay in the construction of responses caused by each service involved. Figure 4 shows the corresponding sequence diagram used to build the answer of the Assistant, in response to the user question "Give me the Current Assets of Petrobras in 2009".

V. Tests And Evaluation Of FVA

For testing the FVA efficiency, the financial domain questions were performed to evaluate the Assistant in relation to the question understanding, the speed of response and its accuracy. Another objective was to evaluate the impact of services in the responses overall time. To standardize the results and facilitate measurements and calculations, a javascript script was created, embedded in a Web page client. This script has submitted a series of 43 questions written in natural language and in English language to the FVA.

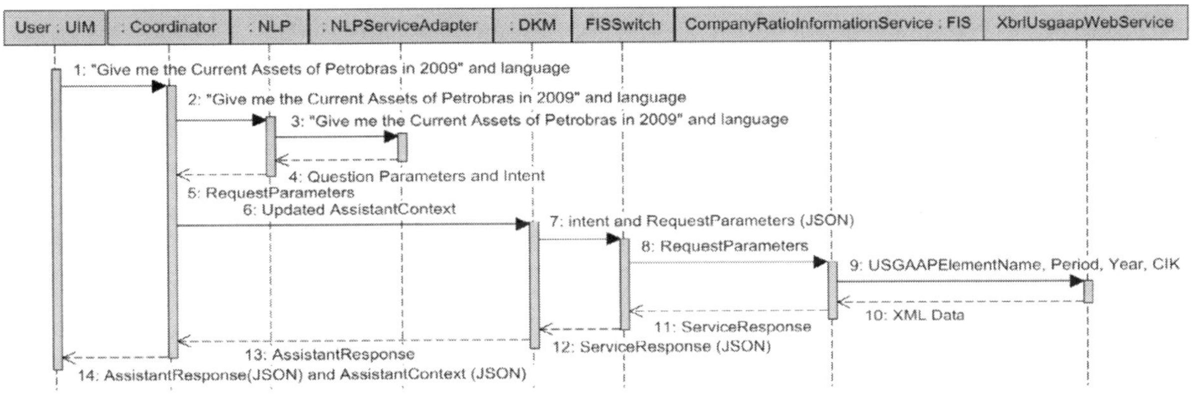

Figure 4. Sequence Diagram of a succesful transaction

As a premise, the key words embedded in the questions of the sequences have been previously registered in the dictionaries of terms and all questions followed the patterns recorded in the NLP grammar. The responses execution times were measured with the same group of questions on different days and at different part of day in order to decrease the impact of the momentary effects caused by network congestion, services overload or processing delay on client computers and/or servers. The tests were performed between June 7th and August 16th 2016 at different times and resulted in 16 samples. For each sample, were measured the individual performance times of the used services and the overall performance of FVA, as shown below: a) total time of Assistant response; b) the response time of Api.ai NLP; c) response time of data service of XBRL-US [17].

The test results showed an average response time equal to 2 seconds, shown in Table 1. These results are compatible with the assistants more used on the market, e.g., Siri, Google Now. The impact of NLP and data services on the average total time Assistant response corresponded to approximately 97%. Any decrease in response times of these services has a directly and significantly impact to the global time, which was evidenced by lower response times recorded for the repeated questions. This decrease is attributed to the use of cache on the data service, which provided a reduction of more than 700 milliseconds on average total time of Assistant. The submitted questions were understood and correctly answered by FVA, in contrast to what happened to the virtual assistants available on the market, which for most of the answers provided it was only a list of links for financial Web sites. Something justifiable, as both Siri and Google Now, do not include the financial domain yet.

To evaluate the management of dialogue with user, a series of four questions was analyzed, three of them are short that were submitted in English language to the Siri, Google Now and FVA. Thus, they were understood and correctly answered by FVA as follows:

1) Submitted question: "Show me the current liabilities of Microsoft in 2014";

2) FVA response: "The Current Liabilities of MICROSOFT CORPORATION Company in 2014 is US$45,625.00";

3) Submitted question: "and 2014";

4) FVA response: "The Current Liabilities of MICROSOFT CORPORATION Company in 2014 is US$45,625.00";

5) Submitted question: "and 2015";

6) FVA response: "The Current Liabilities of MICROSOFT CORPORATION Company in 2015 is US$49,647.00";

7) Submitted question: "and the assets";

8) FVA response: "The Assets of MICROSOFT CORPORATION Company in 2015 is US$174,472.00".

However, the other two assistants understood the following short questions as new questions, as was the case with Siri, illustrated in Figure 5.

The FVA was better than the other two assistants, because it was the only assistant that made the connection between the questions in sequence and managed the dialog. The evaluation of dialog management of the FVA was also considered positive.

VI. CONCLUSION

The positive evaluations of the performance, accuracy tests and dialogue maintaining test, confirmed the viability of the FVA that helps users using natural language, with optional voice support, to obtain information about financial indexes or financial concepts of companies. The proposed architecture for Virtual Assistants can be used to build multilingual virtual assistants for a specific domain that answers user questions through natural language is a contribution of this work; the alternative of consulting financial data that is in electronic reports in XBRL technology and US-GAAP taxonomy, through by natural language, is another contribution.

The US-GAAP taxonomy was used on the FVA implementation, but, with minor changes in the Data layer and changes in the dictionaries and grammar of NLP, it is possible to use others XBRL taxonomies.

Despite the positive results, the FVA has some limitations, e.g., FVA does not recognize any financial questions that are not configured on the NLP. The questions used in the tests were compulsorily chosen according to the

TABLE I. RESPONSE TIMES OF THE FINANCIAL VIRTUAL ASSISTANT

Scope of Measurement	***Global Average of Assistant (ms)***	***Api.ai NLP Average* (ms)**	***XBRL US Service Average* (ms)**	***Api.ai NLP %***	***XBRL US Service %***	***Sum of Serviçes (Api.ai, XBRL US)* (ms)**	***Sum of Serviçes %***
All 43 questions	2011,15	848,29	1115,21	42,18	55,45	1963,50	97,63
Repeated Questions Only	1291,35	833,20	412,83	64,53	31,97	1246,13	96,50
Diference	719,79	14,99	702,38	-22,35	23,48	717,37	1,13

settings made in the grammars and dictionaries of NLP. Any question that is not expected by the Assistant does not bring any relevant information to the user, only a warning that the Assistant did not understand the question.

As future work to improve the FVA we suggest the study of implementation of a component that allows to configure the grammar of the Assistant through a standard language for construction of grammars, e.g., JSpeech Grammar Format [18], and convert this configuration into a proprietary configuration used in NLP. Another suggestion is the creation of an NLP to recognize the financial questions and extract the financial parameters without the need to configure question standards and thus facilitate the expansion of knowledge of the Assistant.

REFERENCES

[1] Apple, SIRI. [Online]. Available from: http://www.apple.com/siri [retrieved: March, 2017].

[2] Microsoft, Cortana. [Online]. Available from: https://developer.microsoft.com/en-us/cortana [retrieved: March, 2017].

[3] Google, Google Now. [Online]. Available from: https://www.google.com/now/ [retrieved: October, 2016].

[4] XBRL International, "The Standard XBRL". [Online] Available from: https://www.xbrl.org/the-standard/ [retrieved: March, 2017].

[5] E. C. Paraiso and J. A. Barthès, "A Voice-Enabled Assistant in a Multi-agent System for e-Government Services," Proc. 5th International School and Symposium, pp. 495-503.

[6] D. B. Lange, "Mobile objects and mobile agents: The future of distributed computing?," Proc. ECOOP'98 - Object-Oriented Programming. Springer-Verlag Berlin Heidelberg. pp. 1-12, 1998.

[7] E. M. Eisman, V. López, and J. L. Castro, "A framework for designing closed domain virtual assistants," Expert Systems With Applications. Granada, Spain, v. 39, n. 3, pp. 3135-3144, 2012

[8] S. P. Zambiasi, "A reference architecture for the personal assistant softwares based on service-oriented architecture." Universidade Federal de Santa Catarina, Florianópolis, Brazil.

[9] SYN, Syn Virtual Assistant. [Online]. Available from: http://syn.co.in/Syn-Virtual-Assistant.aspx [retrieved: November, 2016].

[10] SYN, Syn Engine 2.0. [Online]. Available from: http://syn.co.in/Syn-Engine.aspx [retrieved: September, 2016].

[11] API.AI, Assistant.ai. [Online]. Available from: https://assistant.ai [retrieved: October, 2016].

[12] A. A. Abrāão and P. C. da Silva, "A XBRL Financial Virtual Assistant," Proc. The 11th Conference On Internet And Web Applications And Services, May. 2016, pp. 64-72. ISSN: 2308-3972, ISBN: 978-1-61208-474-9.

[13] API.AI, Api.ai. [Online]. Available from: https://api.ai [retrieved: March, 2017].

[14] ECMA International, ECMA-404: The JSON Data Interchange Format. 1st Geneva, 2013.

[15] U.S. Securities And Exchange Commission, Office of Structured Disclosure.

[16] XBRL US, "US GAAP Financial Reporting Taxonomy," [Online]. Available from: https://xbrl.us/xbrl-taxonomy/2016-us-gaap/ [retrieved: March, 2017].

[17] XBRL US, Data Analysis Toolkit. Available from: https://xbrl.us/home/use/data-analysis-toolkit/ [retrieved: March, 2017].

[18] W3C, JSpeech Grammar Format. [Online]. Available from: https://www.w3.org/TR/jsgf/ [retrieved: March, 2017].

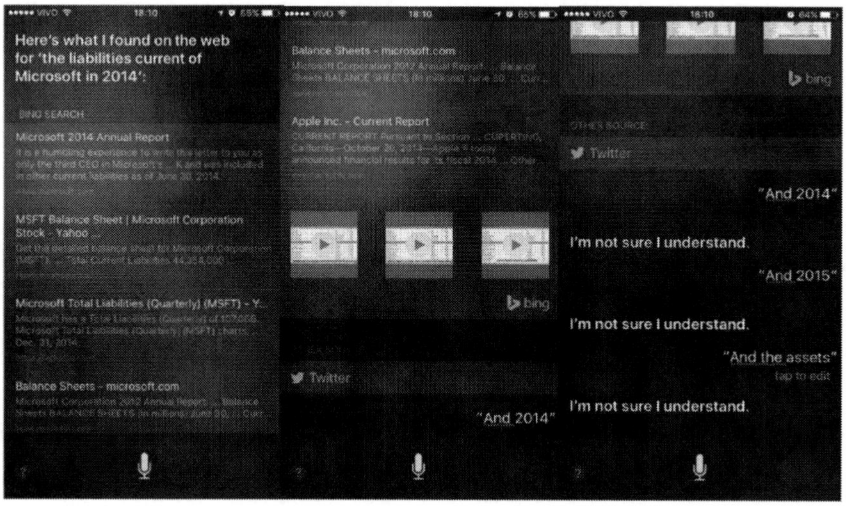

Figure 5. Siri's response to subsequent short questions.

AUTHOR INDEX